Developing Influencing Skills

How to influence people by increasing your credibility, trustworthiness and communication skills

Lots of exercises and case studies
Free downloadable workbook

Deborah Dalley and Lois Burton

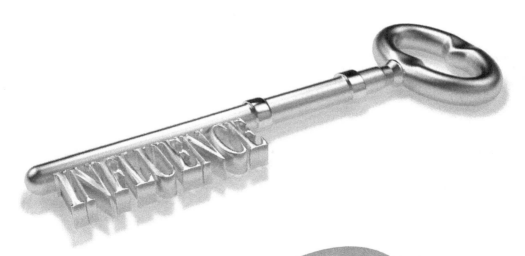

Skills Training Course
www.UoLearn.com

Developing your influencing skills

How to influence people by increasing your credibility, trustworthiness and communication skills

Lots of exercises and case studies, Free downloadable workbook

(Skills training course)

Published by: Universe of Learning Ltd, reg number 6485477, Lancashire, UK
www.UoLearn.com, support@UoLearn.com

First Published 2010

ISBN 978-1-84937-022-6

Other editions:
ebook pdf format 978-1-84937-015-8
ebook epub format 978-1-84937-016-5

Cover picture by Corne-Enroc, Buenos Aires, Argentina, www.Corne.com.ar
Photographs by various artists, © www.fotolia.com
Mountain photo in trait 4: ©Bethany Dalley
Word pictures designed with thanks to www.wordle.net

Proof reading with thanks to Sarah Stansfield.

The poem Risk in trait one has been attributed to several authors. We have been unable to ascertain the correct person or how to pay any royalties owing.
If you can help with this please email editingteam@uolearn.com

About the authors: Lois Burton and Deborah Dalley

Deborah Dalley and Lois Burton both have their roots in the field of learning and development in which they have worked for over 20 years. Both run successful consultancy and coaching businesses and work on many collaborative projects as colleagues and friends.

With backgrounds that span work in the public, private and voluntary sectors Lois and Deborah share many professional interests and values and bring complementary experience to their work.

Deborah and Lois run many workshops and programmes which include the development of influencing skills and together have developed the popular Beyond series of workshops which provide a unique forum for leaders to receive individual, in depth feedback on their impact, presence and ability to influence in a variety of settings.

Deborah Dalley

Deborah Dalley has been working as a freelance training and development consultant for over 20 years. Her employment background is the Criminal Justice System and Higher Education and she has carved a niche as a primary consultant in the Higher Education sector in the North West of England. Deborah is particularly interested in leadership and team development in this sector with much of her work focusing around influencing, emotional intelligence and the management of change.

Deborah's areas of expertise include:

- ✓ Powerful influencing
- ✓ Happiness and motivation
- ✓ Assertive communication
- ✓ Emotional intelligence
- ✓ Leadership and management development
- ✓ Managing change and transition
- ✓ Team development

Deborah has been involved in many major organizational change initiatives and has worked with managers and leadership teams over many years. She brings this experience to bear in her work and has a passionate interest in helping managers to cope with the challenges that constant change bring.

Most recently Deborah has developed a powerful model for holding courageous conversations which helps to remove some of the blocks and barriers to effective communication within organizations.

Please contact Deborah at www.deborahdalley.com

Lois Burton

Lois is a freelance organizational development consultant and leadership coach who has worked in the field of learning and development for 18 years. Since setting up her consultancy in 2000, she has built a reputation as one of the most successful facilitators of organizational change and leadership coaches in the North West of England.

Lois's areas of expertise include:

✓ Powerful influencing

✓ Emotional intelligence

✓ Creating values based culture change

✓ Individual and team coaching

✓ Leadership and management development

Lois is an accredited consultant and coach in Emotional Intelligence for Hay Group Worldwide and is also accredited with the Barrett Values Center for the use of their tools for Corporate Transformation.

Lois is currently working in the area of imagination to unleash new ideas and innovative thinking to reinvigorate organizations and individuals and her new range of products based on the Power of Imagination will soon be available.

She is also part of a group developing ideas on Organizational Transformation working with the Chartered Institute of Personnel and Development (CIPD) and Manchester Business School.

Please contact Lois at www.spherecreativelearning.com

What do people say about influencing skills?

"Very readable book which has changed my perspective on influencing. I always thought of it as a set of tools and techniques but the idea of becoming more influential is much more interesting. This book makes that idea feel possible".

"I liked the whole concept of developing the traits of influential people and really liked the way they were presented. I enjoyed the exercises and have started to influence people in different ways as a result. Thank you for the ideas."

"It has made me realize that perhaps I have put too much effort into influencing external clients and stakeholders and not enough time trying to be influential with my own staff!!"

"I quickly realized that, influencing is a much broader topic than I had imagined. I gained from it an understanding that I stand a better chance of maximizing my effectiveness if I play to my own strengths, rather than trying to meet other's expectations of me."

"Most importantly, I learnt that some of the "influencing" I see employed by others is really manipulations and not only is it not necessary but it can in fact be counterproductive to subscribe to this method. It was very reassuring to hear that I don't have to become someone I'm not in order to extend my influence!"

Contents

CONTENTS

Introduction:
Developing your influencing skills

"Influence is not only held by people in authority,
any one of us can learn to become more influential
in our lives and work."

Lois Burton and Deborah Dalley

Introduction:
Developing your influencing skills

When you think of someone influential who comes to mind?

Is it famous names like Nelson Mandela, Barack Obama, Bill Gates – people who are on the global stage affecting the world, or is it someone you know at work – a chief executive, director, manager, leader in your organization? Is it a teacher, doctor, carer – someone who powerfully affects your life at a deeper level or indeed a member of your family or a friend – someone who makes your life better? Or do you think of yourself?

We all have our own ideas about who we see as being influential but what characteristics make these people stand out?
The answer to the above question is what this book is all about.

For the last twenty years we have worked with individuals and groups looking at the skills of influencing. Influencing is one of our most powerful tools to succeed in both our careers and lives. As we have worked with people on this topic two key things have emerged:

Firstly, the notion that becoming more influential is more than picking up a set of specific influencing tools and techniques.

Secondly, that there are certain traits that influential people have in common and these can be developed.

This book will explain what those traits are. In the following chapters we will describe each of the traits, provide case studies and exercises to enable you to explore and reflect on these traits and help you to develop your personal action plan to becoming more influential.

Who is this book for?

This book has been written with several audiences in mind – it could be used by:

✓ Individuals who are interested in assessing and developing their personal influence

✓ Learning professionals who want to use the exercises with groups in their training sessions

✓ Managers or coaches who can use many of the exercises to help an individual to think through ways to increase their influence

✓ Managers who want to develop a more influential leadership style

How to use this book

Following the introductory chapter this book is divided into seven parts. Each section covers one of the traits and aims to:

➢ Describe the trait and help you to recognize whether you currently demonstrate those behaviors

➢ Provide guidance and exercises on ways to develop the characteristics of each trait further

There is no particular order to the traits so you can use this book in any way that you want. Read it from cover to cover or dip in at any point that interests you.

At the end of each chapter we have listed a number of websites and books that you may find useful if you wish to do further reading on the topics described in that chapter. At the end of the book there is an action plan. This is somewhere that you can record any thoughts about things you want to do in order to become more influential.

If you visit our website www.UoLearn.com then you will find a free downloadable workbook with all the exercises from this books and plenty of space to write.

What are the 7 traits?

Over the years we have worked in the field of personal development it has become increasingly evident that influencing is not an exact science, it is an art. It is not a set of manipulative tools and techniques that can be learned on a one day course, it is a way of being – a set of beliefs and behaviors that are evident in the way an individual conducts both their professional and private lives.

We have identified seven traits that are shared by influential people:

> **Knowing what you want and believing that you can get it.**
  Being clear about our sense of purpose and goals is the first step to becoming more influential.

> **Credibility**
  This is about how believable we are to other people. Our credibility with someone comes from three things the reputation we have, how they perceive our expertise and what has happened in the past.

> **Trustworthiness**
  This is a fundamental element of influence. We are more open to be influenced by someone that we trust and we are more inclined to trust people who we think are authentic. This is often described as being the same on the outside as on the inside. The most influential leaders are those who operate from values such as truth, trust and integrity and use those values with the intent to benefit not just themselves but the people around them as well.

> **Strong Communication Capability**
  However self aware, genuine and honest we are, the ability to get others to follow comes from our capacity to communicate effectively. Highly influential people are usually articulate, willing and able to listen and often charismatic. They are also aware of their impact and the effect they have on others.

> **Empathy**
  It is important to remember that we will never influence someone from our point of view. The ability to step away from our personal viewpoint and explore someone else's perception of the world is essential.

> **Inspirational**
  Enthusiasm is infectious. We have all experienced how contagious negative emotion can be and it is equally true of positive energy. Inspiring others involves motivating and capturing their imagination. Martin Luther King used powerful imagery in his famous "I have a dream" speech – the picture he painted and the feelings it evoked did far more to capture the imagination and influence others than a factual account would have done.

> **Open-Mindedness**
  Flexibility and a willingness to embrace change are also traits that are evident in most influential people.

Goals and beliefs

Open-mindedness   Credibility

7 traits

Inspirational   Trustworthiness

Empathy   Communication capability

The difference between influence and manipulation

We want to start by clarifying the differences between becoming more influential and influencing by manipulation.

Does becoming more influential mean becoming an expert in the art of manipulating others to get what you want? In our experience as training providers over a number of years, this is the question that we have often debated with our delegates.

This question creates a tension in many people as they don't want to feel manipulative, however, they do want to feel able to both convince and persuade others. It doesn't help that many role models seen as being influential both in organizational and public life are also seen as manipulative – masters of spin. The other difficulty is that many people see these tactics working for those who use them and have few examples of other ways of influencing that are equally successful.

We are looking to show a different way for those who wish to become more influential but do not wish to become more manipulative. Our intention is firstly, to challenge the premise that manipulation truly succeeds in any sustainable way and to look at the differences between influence and manipulation.

Manipulation is defined as:
"To manage or control artfully or by shrewd use of influence, often in an unfair or fraudulent way."

By contrast, influence is defined as:
"A power affecting a person, thing, or course of events, especially one that operates without any direct or apparent effort."

It is very clear within these definitions that manipulation, whilst seen as shrewd, also has the elements of unfairness and fraudulence within it whilst influence is concerned with a powerful effect but does not need to carry the darker side of manipulation within it.

Some of the influencing tactics and techniques we have seen taught on training courses can appear to be effective in the short term however they often carry inherent pitfalls because they can be seen as being manipulative.

So what are those pitfalls?

First and foremost, there may be a loss of self confidence and trust in yourself. If you are constantly looking for ways to win in situations then you focus only on undermining the views of others and lose your sense of integrity and identity in the process. If you look at some of the public figures who have been caught in manipulative practises all have eventually become run by their own fear and insecurity and in the process have lost their confidence and thus their power and impact. Some recover, but many never do.

Secondly, you may lose the confidence and trust of others. At work and at home we are often trying to influence the same people time and time again. If someone feels that you have tried to manipulate them or outmaneuver them in the past the trust between you will be diminished. Trust takes a long time to build but can be lost in a moment. Once lost, it takes even longer to build again and without it our capacity to influence that person is significantly reduced.

Thirdly, the loss of the end goal. Machiavelli propounded the principle that the end justifies the means. This is the seduction that leads many down the manipulative path – if I am looking at an end that is inherently right, am I not justified in a little manipulation to get there? Time and time again this has been proven to be a false principle – the means nearly always impact the end goal and an end goal gained by manipulation never maintains its original integrity.

Trait 1:

Knowing what you want and believing you can achieve it.

"Believe and act as if it were impossible to fail."
Charles Kettering

Trait 1:
Knowing what you want and believing you can achieve it

In this section we will be:

✓ Defining the trait

✓ Clarifying the importance of developing a strong sense of purpose and clear goals

✓ Explaining the importance of articulating those goals in a positive way i.e. saying what you want as opposed to what you don't want!

✓ Exploring how to build your belief in your ability to achieve your goals through developing self belief, considered risk taking and resilience

"Let him who would move the world, first move himself." Socrates

What do we mean by knowing what you want and believing you can achieve it?

It is important to define our starting point, an initial trait which we believe is fundamental to influential people is knowing what you want AND believing you are going to get it.

What we mean by this is, a strong sense of purpose, clear goals around that purpose and your belief in your ability to achieve it. These are the building blocks to increasing your influence. All of the influential people we have observed exhibit this trait.

Sense of purpose and clear goals

There are hundreds (probably thousands) of books and tapes on self development that will stress the importance of clear goals. What we have observed in highly influential people is that they not only have clear goals – they also have a clearly defined sense of purpose. This gives them a direction and context in which to operate. Having a defined sense of purpose gives energy and meaning to your goals. This is the reason that we are including both within this book – we see these as the twin foundation stones to increasing your influence.

Other people respond to this clear and deep seated sense of purpose and goals.

One of the reasons this is so attractive is that many of us find defining our sense of purpose and goals quite challenging. Often we have been defined by other people's expectations and goals and have never really connected to our own.

We have worked with many people over the years who have struggled to identify what they are really trying to achieve.

*"If you don't know where you are going
you will probably end up somewhere else."*
Laurence Peter

Some common dilemmas that people have brought to training sessions or coaching include:

➢ Do I want to be the best teacher/lawyer/nurse in the profession and practice my craft
  or do I want to manage the process and move up through the organization?

➢ Do I know what I want from my life
  or do I follow the things that others expect from me?

➢ Do I work to live
  or live to work?

➢ Do I want to influence this decision because it will be good for my career
  or because I truly believe it is the right thing to do?

Do any of these sound familiar?

If you are struggling with this type of dilemma then it directly impacts your ability to set goals with any sense of clarity. You are unable to decide which goal is the right one to set or will be trying subconsciously to meet two different and sometimes conflicting goals. Developing a sense of purpose can be seen as slightly removed from the pragmatic world of work that most of us operate in. However, we believe that the lack of this is one of most common reasons for lack of influence and working on this area can dramatically increase capacity to become more influential.

The starting point to build a foundation from which to influence is to ask yourself, "What do I really want to happen and for what reason?" This can relate to our lives as a whole or to a particular area in which we want to influence the outcome.

In order to do this, we have to acknowledge that we have both the right and responsibility to take control of our own lives rather than being defined by other people's expectations. Influential people are not defined by others, they forge their own path.

Tips to develop goals and a clear sense of purpose:

✓ **Be prepared to spend time on this** – many people when asked what their goals are, say "I don't know, I've never known, things just happen, don't they, and then you make the best of them." This is simply not good enough. If you want to influence what happens in your life and career you need to be prepared to spend time working out your goals as you would work on any plan.

✓ **Get help** – there are numerous books and exercises devoted solely to goal setting. If you cannot do this alone, get a coach who can work with you.

✓ **Start small if you are struggling** – this is direct contradiction to some of the advice on goal setting which says always look at whatever your whole life goals are and work back from there.

From our experience if someone has never thought about what they want before – looking at the whole life plan can be too big and people become paralyzed. So, start with what you want in a small way and work up.

Case Study

One of the delegates on a recent training course started with what he enjoyed in his current job and would not want to lose. We looked at a very specific goal which was around his next job containing opportunities to do more research based activity and less teaching.

He then set a goal to have a conversation with his manager to see if he could adjust the balance slightly in his current role to prepare him better for the next step. He achieved this goal within a fortnight, which then gave him confidence to move onto saying that his ultimate goal was to do research full time, and also to develop a working pattern that gave him more flexibility so he could do more work from home and travel less for work.

He set a two year time span for this and from there had conversations which started to push him in the right direction. This example of starting small meant that this delegate could move onto the bigger picture as a result, whereas in that first session, he simply could not envision the bigger picture.

Exercise: Goal Setting

Think about your current job (or situation if you do not currently have a job).
What is it that you most enjoy at the moment?
What would you like more of?

Identify one action that will help you get more of what you enjoy and state it as a goal i.e.

My goal is to create more

....

....

....

in my job or current situation.

Next identify one action that will influence that goal and bring it nearer

My action is

....

....

....

I commit to taking this action by

....

Once you have achieved one goal it gives you confidence to go on from there. Do this exercise again once you have achieved your first goal and start to expand your horizons. You are on the path to becoming more influential in your own life and with others.

Articulating your goals in a positive way

Having goals is one thing, articulating those goals is different again. It is surprising just how many people when asked what they want are less than clear in their reply.

From our experience it is much easier for people to say what they don't want rather than what they do. Stating your goals in the negative i.e. from the perspective of what you don't want is not an influential trait. It gives a negative impression and is also frustrating – to become more influential it is essential that your starting point is clarity about what you do want.

It is very easy to start your influencing in the wrong way if you have not defined what you want in the first place.

Consider the following case study which was brought forward as an influencing problem in a coaching session.

Case Study

The coachee was one of 3 senior team leaders in a high profile department, which was undergoing a restructure.

Her starting point was:

My department is undergoing a restructure and I want to influence how my team is structured. At present, I am not part of the decision making group although one of my colleagues, who is a team leader in exactly the same position as I am, is part of the group. I feel very frustrated by this situation.

I have told my boss that I don't want my team to be structured in exactly the same way as my colleagues as we have a different role and need a different structure. I think it could be a real problem and I am worried about it. What I think could happen is that decisions will be made which are not right for my team and what I don't want is for that to happen and we then have to start unpicking those decisions.

All my boss said to me was that I didn't need to worry because the needs of all the different teams will be taken into consideration by the decision making group but he appreciated my concern and would make sure that this point was reinforced.

This was not the response I wanted at all. I feel even more frustrated now because I still think that my concerns are justified and I don't believe that anyone who doesn't work in the team will have a full understanding of what we need.

Does this ring any bells for you?

This is an all too familiar scenario from which someone starts their influencing process by stating what they don't want rather than what they do want and inevitably gets the response they don't want! Talking about what you don't want invites confusion as in the above scenario.

The coachee's manager was completely unclear about what she wanted. The manager answered what he assumed was the question he had been asked.

I.e. "How will the decisions be made and can I be sure that my team's role will be taken into consideration?"

Actually the question was, "May I be part of the decision making group as I believe that my contribution would be vital to ensuring my team is structured in the right way?"

Feel the difference if someone starts with what they do want and frames the request clearly. This is not to say that the first answer you get will always be the one which you want, however, at least you start in the right place.

Influential people always start in the right place. They are not afraid to ask for what they want clearly and directly. You are then in the position to build on that.

In this instance we worked on how this coachee could set up another conversation in which she clarified with her manager, what she wanted. It worked. Her manager had assumed that the coachee was too busy to be part of the group and had therefore, given the role to her colleague whose workload was slightly less. After a much more constructive discussion both she and the third team leader were invited to be part of the decision making group.

Exercise: How clearly do you state your goals?

Think about a situation in which you want to influence more strongly:-

First, write down the present situation and the way(s) you have been dealing with it, being as honest as you can so that you can check if you are falling into the "don't want" trap.

....

....

....

....

....

....

Secondly, write down your goal/exactly what you want out of the situation as clearly as possible.

....

....

....

....

....

....

....

Make sure that you have written your goals in a positive way - have you stated what you want?

You now have your starting point!

Practice this skill in all situations in which you want to increase your influence. You must be clear at the outset to have any chance of influencing strongly.

Believing you can achieve your goals

Influential people not only know what they want, **they believe strongly in their own ability to get it.**

There are 3 parts to strengthening your belief in your ability to achieve your goals:

- ✓ **Self belief**
- ✓ **Considered risk taking**
- ✓ **Resilience**

Influential people understand the importance of belief in themselves. They also have a willingness to step out of their comfort zones, take some risks and the resilience to bounce back from setbacks. We rarely achieve our goals without meeting some obstacles.

Influential people hold onto their goals in the face of setbacks and have the resilience to get straight back in the game.

Self belief

Is sounds self evident, but what is self belief and how do we foster it?

Self belief is the inner confidence that you will succeed and that you can overcome obstacles to achieve your goals.

How can we foster our self belief?
Focusing on the best rather than the worst is the key.

Exercise: Successful times

Make a list of all the times you have successfully influenced situations in your life.

....

....

....

....

....

....

Write down what you did that helped that process:

....

....

....

....

....

....

Keep that list easily accessible so that you can focus on those occasions rather than on times when you have been unsuccessful. Focusing on our best times rather than our worst times helps to foster self belief.

We can strengthen our self belief by the willingness to focus on positive characteristics rather than negative and acknowledging the fact that our own negative self talk, our inner critic is the biggest enemy of our self belief. When we listen too strongly to our inner critic it saps our self belief and paralyzes our ability to believe that we can achieve our goals. As with the don't want trap, there is also a won't get trap!

Another enemy of self belief is fear of failure, which we explore in more detail in the risk taking section. Because we fear failure many people will not try in the first place. The faulty thinking goes something like this, "It's not worth trying because I probably won't succeed and if I don't succeed when I have tried really hard then I will feel worse than I do now!"

Many people will not take action/ask for what they want because they make the assumption that they will not get it, therefore there is no point in asking. This saves them from having to face up to a potential set back, which often gets labelled as failure. Yet, few people succeed in anything important the first time – influential people accept this and cultivate the resilience to deal with it. On being asked about how it felt to fail 2,000 times when he was working on the invention of the light bulb, Thomas Edison said:

> *"I never failed, I invented the light bulb,*
> *it was a 2,000 stage process."*

Beware not only of the "don't want" mindset but of the "won't get" mindset. Won't get becomes a self fulfilling prophecy - we assume we won't get, therefore, we don't ask or we ask in the wrong way, therefore we don't get, therefore our self belief goes down and next time we make the same assumption of won't get from an even more negative mindset. This drains our influence completely.

If you take the previous case study as an example, that person had assumed that there was some kind of problem with her belonging to the group. She did not know the real reason, so built her own fantasy that there was no point in asking directly, as obviously she wouldn't get the right answer. She therefore asked the wrong question and her self fulfilling prophecy came true.

We have to break the mind set of won't get to increase our influence!

Our won't get (don't deserve to get) voice sounds something like this:

- ✘ My needs are not as important as theirs.
- ✘ They won't like my ideas.
- ✘ Should I say something or will that look as if I am interfering?
- ✘ If it doesn't work out it will look as though I have failed.
- ✘ I will feel really embarrassed if others do not agree.
- ✘ Maybe I am wrong.
- ✘ It will be an uphill battle to get others to agree and I'm not sure if I have the energy.

In order to combat our won't get voice we have to be able to access thoughts that create a will get mindset. The will get mindset is at the heart of self belief.

Our will get voice would sound something like this:

- ✓ I value my needs as much as the needs of others.
- ✓ I know my ideas are good and I believe other people will think so too.
- ✓ I want to help and therefore, I need to say something.
- ✓ If it doesn't work out – at least I know I have tried.
- ✓ If others don't agree we can talk about it – it means I will have opened up the dialogue.
- ✓ What if I'm right?
- ✓ This is important to me, therefore, I know I will find the energy to influence others and I do have lots of support to draw on.
- ✓ If at first you don't succeed.......................
- ✓ I know I can achieve this – I just need to find the right way to go about it.

Imagine, focus, believe and keep going!

Taking risks

The ability to develop a will get mindset does mean that we have to be prepared to take some risks. Risk is part of growth. If we look at truly influential people in the world they have all been willing to follow their vision and goals even if that has involved an element of risk. Very few people succeed without taking risks and learning from setbacks. One of the problems with an increasingly litigious culture is that we strive to eliminate risk. This can and often does paralyze people – we have watched many managers lose the belief and loyalty of their staff because they have become unable to take a decision. We have to be able to step out of our comfort zone and live with a degree of uncertainty.

Taking calculated risks is very different from acting rashly, it is about accepting that sometimes we have to take action without being totally sure that nothing can go wrong or be lost.

Risks

To laugh is to risk appearing the fool.
To weep is to risk appearing sentimental.
To reach out to another is to risk involvement.
To expose feelings is to risk exposing your true self.
To place your dreams, ideas before a crowd is to risk their loss.
To love is to risk not being loved in return.
To live is to risk dying. To hope is to risk despair.
To try is to risk failure.
But risks must be taken, because the greatest hazard in life is to risk nothing.
The person who risks nothing, does nothing, has nothing and is nothing.
They may avoid suffering and sorrow, but they cannot learn, feel, change, grow, love, live.
Chained by their certitudes, they are a slave:
they have forfeited their freedom.
Only a person who risks is truly free.   *[unattributed]*

As we discussed earlier in self belief, fear is behind most of our difficulties with taking risk. Many fears are irrational but nonetheless very real and difficult to overcome. Starting to deal with our fears is an essential element of being able to take the right amount of risk.

Exercise:
Avoiding being trapped by irrational fears and beliefs

Identify an occasion when you felt unable to try something different or take a risk and then identify what you were afraid what might happen as a result. Was this a rational fear or an irrational one? E.g. I wanted to introduce a new system at work but was afraid I would look foolish if it didn't work.

This type of fear is very common and you need to challenge that idea that you will look foolish. It is often more foolish not to try a new idea and if you have thought it out thoroughly many people will applaud you for trying to improve something. Doing nothing does not serve you or increase your influence.

Identify an occasion like this from your own experience.

Occasion I felt unable to take a risk:

....
....
....

What I was afraid might happen as a result:

....
....
....

Challenge the fear that was behind your inability to take a risk and see if you can reframe it for yourself. Write down what you will do differently next time – if you are struggling with this have a look at the tips at the end of this chapter or try reading a book on building self confidence.
What will I do differently next time?

....
....
....

Resilience

To be resilient means to be able to "spring back" into shape. To be emotionally resilient means to be able to spring back emotionally after suffering through difficult and stressful times in one's life. Stressed people experience a flood of powerful negative emotions which may include anger, anxiety, and depression. Some people remain trapped in these negative emotions long after the stressful events that have caused them have passed. Emotionally resilient people, on the other hand, are quickly able to bounce back to their normal emotional state.

Resilience and the ability to bounce back from setbacks is another aspect of believing you can achieve your goals. Few people achieve their goals immediately, and those who throw in their hand after a setback diminish their influence. If your self belief is strong this strengthens your resilience and increases your chance of achievement. All of the most influential figures in history have recognized the importance of resilience and practiced it.

When Thomas Edison's factory was burned down with much of his work lost he said:

"There is a great value in disaster. All our mistakes are burned up. Thank God we can start anew."

Increasing your influence does mean increasing your resilience.

Tips to build your resilience and self belief:

- ✓ List 3 reasons why your views are valued and valuable.
- ✓ Create a support network that can help and encourage you; cheerleaders are very important.
- ✓ Combat stress, stress is the enemy of resilience.
- ✓ Read motivational books and articles.
- ✓ Watch motivational films.
- ✓ Avoid "awfulizing" – letting your thoughts about how awful you or the situation are to spiral out of control.
- ✓ List all the positive things about yourself (we tend to dwell on the negative).
- ✓ If other people praise you, accept it as real.
- ✓ Practice visualizing success, not failure.
- ✓ Use positive language
  - ‣ I will...... not I should
  - ‣ I am going to.........not I will try to
  - ‣ I could if.............not I can't because
- ✓ Congratulate yourself when things go well.
- ✓ If you have a problem that you can do something about, do it – if you cannot do anything about it then incorporate it into your plans rather than keep wishing that it was different.
- ✓ Acknowledge and learn from your mistakes but do not spend a lot of time or energy blaming yourself or others.

Exercise: Your support network

List your support network - include only people who foster your self belief rather than undermine you.

....
....
....

If your list is quite small, think about how you could expand your support network e.g. join a club or business network. List your ideas:

....
....
....

Summary of trait 1:
Knowing what you want and believing that you can achieve it

In summary, to develop this trait concentrate on:

- ✓ Developing your sense of purpose and clarifying your goals remember to start small if you are struggling
- ✓ Avoid defining yourself by the expectations of others
- ✓ Articulate your goals clearly
- ✓ Focus on what you do want not what you don't want. Avoid the "don't want" trap
- ✓ Remember Edison – cultivate resilience
- ✓ Get a strong support network
- ✓ Beat the "won't get" mind set: it is totally possible to change a mind set
- ✓ Be willing to step out of your comfort zone and take a risk

Further Reading:

Feel the Fear and Do It Anyway, Susan Jeffers, Vermillion, 978-0091907075

The Self Esteem Workbook, Lynda Field, Vermillion, 978-0091857332

www.mygoals.com

www.businessballs.com/goal_planning.htm

www.valuescentre.com

Trait 2:
Credibility

"We judge ourselves by what we feel capable of doing, while others judge us by what we have already done."

Henry Longfellow

Trait 2:
Credibility

In this section we will be:

- ✓ Defining what credibility means
- ✓ Examining how to assess your credibility rating with people
- ✓ Exploring how your reputation may affect your credibility
- ✓ Identifying ways to build your reputation
- ✓ Listing ways to develop your expertise and capability in order to be more credible
- ✓ Helping you to develop your ability to deliver what you promise

"The more you are willing to accept responsibility for your actions, the more credibility you will have." Brian Koslow

What is credibility?

Credibility is a critical element in how influential we are. It is quite a difficult thing to define so let's begin with several dictionary definitions:

"The quality, capability or power to elicit belief."
"The quality of being believable and trustworthy."
"A reputation impacting on one's ability to be believed."

These definitions clearly demonstrate that credibility is not something we can assess about ourselves. It is something that other people perceive about us.

Exercise: Who do you think is credible?

Spend a few minutes identifying someone you know who you consider to be credible.

....

What are the key things about that person that made you choose them?

....

....

....

....

....

Some examples that people have given when answering this question include:

"I have identified my doctor as someone I consider to be credible. This is because I respect the knowledge and experience that she has and I have had very good advice from her in the past."

"My first manager stands out for me – he was always honest and open with me and if he said he was going to do something he did."

"I think the professor I work for is very credible – he is an expert in his field and has published many books. You often see his name quoted in things like the Lancet."

Your answer may not be the same as these however it probably does relate to at least one of the following:

➢ The capability of the individual
➢ The relationship you have with the person
➢ What other people have told you about them
➢ Their reputation
➢ Their qualifications or experience
➢ What has happened in the past between you and them

The key is to recognize that credibility can be developed, it might take some work, but it can be done. Invest your time and energy in doing the things that will achieve that, not in concentrating on things that you cannot do anything about. The following case study demonstrates how sometimes we lose sight of the things that we can actively do to increase our credibility.

Case Study

Sarah was a 28 year old graduate who had been working for the organization for about 3 months. She was extremely energetic and I had been very impressed with the contribution she had made to the team. During her first personal development review I asked her how well she felt she had settled into the organization. She said that she was finding it very difficult to work in such a male dominated environment. She felt that people beyond the team did not take her seriously because she was young and female. She cited several examples of meetings in which she believed she had failed to influence the outcome because people did not believe she was old enough to be credible. We discussed the effect this was having on her work and she admitted that she was investing a lot of energy and time in dwelling on the unfairness of that perception. This had resulted in her becoming quite defensive and not contributing as much as she had when first appointed.

She quickly recognized that this was not a particularly productive path to follow and so decided to harness that time and energy in doing things that would increase her credibility. She began to build strong relationships within the organization, establish a reputation for delivering results and spent a lot of time on her own personal development.
A year later Sarah was promoted!

This is a very common story, we often connect others perception of our credibility to an issue that we cannot do anything about such as age, gender or educational background. It is undoubtedly true that some organizational cultures do attach credibility to things like experience or length of service. However, dwelling on these causes us to develop a victim status. It is important to recognize how destructive this is. If I am willing to accept that a group of people will not listen to me because I am female, or because of some other factor I cannot alter, then this will quickly become a self fulfilling prophecy.

How credible we are comes essentially from three things – our expertise, our reputation and our track record with someone. It is important to differentiate between reputation in the wider world and direct experience of someone. How often have you heard people say things like, "well loads of people complain about her but she has always been really helpful when I have asked her for something." If we establish a reputation for knowing what we are talking about, being honest, and delivering what we promise then our ability to elicit belief in others grows.

Increasing your credibility

As previously mentioned it is tricky to assess your own credibility because it is not something we can tell about ourselves. However it can be useful to stop and think about the person you are trying to influence and try to gauge what they think about you – the following questions can help you to do that.

What is this person likely to know about my reputation?

➢ Where will they have heard my name mentioned?
➢ Who is likely to have talked to them about me?
➢ Do we share any acquaintances/work colleagues?
➢ What would they find out if they Googled me?

What experience has this person had of dealing with me?

➢ Have I tried to influence them in the past?

If our credibility rating is low with an individual we are going to have to work much harder to influence them successfully.

Developing your credibility is not something that can be done over night. It does take work, however there is no doubt that people are more likely to be influenced by someone that they consider credible so the work does get rewarded! The following exercises will help you to think of ways to improve the three key components of increasing your credibility:

✓ **Your reputation**

✓ **Your expertise**

✓ **Your ability to deliver**

Building your reputation

All the things that have been discussed so far in this chapter rely on people knowing enough about you to make a decision about your credibility. A key area you can therefore work on in becoming more influential is building and developing your reputation.

Tips for building your reputation:

- ➢ Go to conferences and training courses and talk to a variety of people.
- ➢ Offer to present at conferences and meetings.
- ➢ Prepare well for meetings and research areas you want to talk about.
- ➢ Join on line discussion groups.
- ➢ Social networking – this can also have a negative effect on your reputation. Check that there is nothing on yours or other people's social networking sites that you wouldn't be happy for work colleagues to see.
- ➢ Keep in touch - send interesting articles or other information to people.
- ➢ Focus on other people's needs – do things for others without expecting anything in return.
- ➢ Offer to join working groups.
- ➢ Arrive at meetings a bit early to talk to people.
- ➢ Don't automatically send an e-mail – pick up the phone or arrange to meet.
- ➢ Write articles for in house publications.
- ➢ Publicize your good work.
- ➢ Present an image of a positive thinker.

> ### Exercise: Building your reputation
>
> Identify three things you are going to do to build your reputation at work:
>
> 1 ....
>
> 2 ....
>
> 3 ....

Developing your expertise

There are many activities both at work and in life that can provide opportunities for learning. When we think about ways to develop our knowledge and skills we are often only consider courses and other formal development routes.

The following list highlights 25 ways that we can learn new skills or knowledge:

- Training courses
- Conferences
- Coaching
- Delegation
- Job rotation
- Secondment
- Job shadowing
- Giving presentations
- Deputizing
- Sitting on working parties
- Reading
- On line tutorials
- Internet research
- Trade journals
- Trade exhibitions
- Evening classes
- Mentor
- Attending meetings
- Chairing meetings
- Writing reports
- DVDs and videos
- Project work
- Action learning groups
- Networking
- Audio tapes

Exercise: Your expertise

What other activities have you used to develop yourself over the past 2 years?

....

....

....

Exercise: Developing your expertise

Think about an area of knowledge or skill that you would like to develop. This could be work related or something you would like to do outside work. Once you have identified the area for development decide how you are going to meet that need.

Examples:
I would like to develop better time management skills.
I am going to do this by:
> Talking to and observing my line manager who is excellent at managing her time.
> Buying a book on time management that has been recommended to me.
> Attending the organization's half day time management course

I would like to learn to speak French.
I am going to do this by:
> Borrowing a set of audio CDs from the library
> Attending an evening French speaking class
> Getting a French pen pal

Choose an activity that you think will really enhance your expertise:

I would like to:

....

I am going to do this by:

....
....
....
....

Improving your ability to deliver

However strong your reputation and expertise are it is still not enough if you do not do what you say you will.

As FedEx famously stated –
"A promise is nothing until it is delivered."

What stops you from delivering?

This is a question we have asked in many training workshops and the reasons given are varied. These have included:

- ✗ "Other people have not provided me with information I need to get the job done."
- ✗ "I do not have the right equipment to do the job properly so I won't do it at all."
- ✗ "I didn't have enough time."
- ✗ "I did not really understand what was expected."
- ✗ "I don't like doing things like this."
- ✗ "I need someone to help me with it."
- ✗ "If it goes wrong people will judge me."

It is important to concentrate on ways to overcome these obstacles by focusing on what we could have done differently rather than looking for things or people to blame!

Exercise: Improving your ability to deliver

Think about the last time you did not manage to deliver a task or project on time – what were the reasons?

....

....

....

What could you have done differently?

....

....

....

Tips to develop your time and project management skills:

✓ Develop systems to plan, organize and prioritize your work. This could include to do lists, effective diary management, year planners and filing systems.

✓ Know when you have the most energy during the day and plan to do the hardest tasks then. Most people are at their mental and physical best in the morning.

✓ Learn to say no to jobs that are not yours.

✓ Develop your skills in areas such as speed reading and report writing.

✓ Look at your to do list each day and tackle the thing that you are resisting the most first. Once you have done that task everything else seems easier in comparison!

✓ Restrict interruptions by fixing time limits, meeting in the other person's office or remaining standing during the conversation.

✓ Break projects down into manageable parts and then set yourself interim deadlines. This helps to keep larger tasks moving forward.

Summary of trait 2: Credibility

In summary, to develop this trait, concentrate on:

✓ Thinking about ways to develop your reputation within the organization and the wider community

✓ Ensuring that your expertise is up to date and that you are constantly growing and developing

✓ Putting in systems and processes that ensure that you can deliver what you have promised on time

Further Reading:

Get Everything Done and Still Have Time to Play, Mark Forster, Hodder and Stoughton, 978-0340746202

The Mind Gym: Give Me Time, Time Warner, 978-0316731690

Project Management Pocketbook, Keith Posner and Mike Applegarth, Pocketbooks, 978-1903776872

www.projectagency.com

www.cipd.co.uk

Trait 3:
Trustworthiness

"When people honor each other, there is a trust established that leads to synergy, interdependence and deep respect. Both parties make decisions and choices based on what is right, what is best and what is valued most highly."

Blaine Lee

Trait 3:
Trustworthiness

In this section we will be:

- ✓ Defining what trustworthiness means
- ✓ Examining why authenticity is an important element of trust
- ✓ Exploring how knowing what we value helps us to be more authentic
- ✓ Reviewing the importance of intent
- ✓ Identifying the behaviors that generate trust
- ✓ Looking at ways to develop our communication networks and develop stronger relationships

"If you tell the truth you do not have to remember anything."
Mark Twain

What is trustworthiness?

When people talk about trustworthiness they use words like responsible, honest, reliable, accountable, ethical and integrity, and these are fundamental elements of becoming more influential. In many ways trustworthiness is similar to some of the areas discussed in the previous section on credibility.

However, there is a key difference between the two. Credibility may be gained in a particular area of expertise whereas trusting someone means having confidence in them as a person. An essential characteristic of trust is its reciprocal nature – you only get it if you give it. It can take a long time to build trust and yet it can be destroyed very quickly.

"Trust is like a vase once it is broken, though you can fix it, the vase will never be the same again."

We are far more likely to listen and give consideration to the views of people that we trust than people that we don't. This means that we are more open to be influenced by someone that we trust. Have you ever questioned or challenged someone's viewpoint not because of the quality of the idea, but because of a distrust of the person delivering it?

Authenticity

"No one man can, for any considerable time, wear one face to himself and another to the multitude without finally getting bewildered as to the true one." Hawthorne

We trust people who behave authentically – authenticity happens when we match our ideas and values to the behaviors we exhibit. This is often described as being the same on the outside as on the inside. The following shows how a lack of authenticity did reduce one manager's ability to influence.

Case Study

Many years ago I worked for a manager who told me during my induction that he had an "open door policy". He explained the importance he placed on developing strong working relationships with his staff and that he valued openness and honesty. I was very encouraged by this and was looking forward to working with him and learning from him. However as the months progressed I realized that the reality was his door was never open. If I passed him in the corridor he always said hello but did not stop walking. Difficult messages were always sent to me by e-mail. Meetings were arranged and then cancelled often at short notice. If I needed help or advice it was almost impossible to get. The behavior he exhibited was totally at odds with the things that he had said. In the end I stopped trying to consult with him and began to find ways to work round him – this resulted in distrust on both sides. The relationship quickly deteriorated and I left the department a year later.

This case study demonstrates how important authenticity is in generating trust. It is why self-awareness is such an important part of becoming more influential – we cannot behave authentically without first understanding who we are and what we believe in.

This means being clear about what our values are and using them as the basis of our decision making.

What are values?

The dictionary definition is that values are a collection of guiding, usually positive principles which one deems to be correct and desirable in life, especially regarding personal conduct.

Examples of values may include things like:

➢ Caring

➢ Enthusiasm

➢ Compassion

➢ Optimism

➢ Honesty

➢ Family

➢ Success

➢ Health

Many of us will state that something is really important to us. However, that does not actually translate into practise.

Case Study

During a course on life/work balance one of the delegates realized that she had fallen into that trap. Although she would happily state that one of the things she valued the most was her family, the reality was that she was not demonstrating that. She told us that she was spending a lot of time working and even when she was at home she knew that her attention and focus were often elsewhere. She decided that she needed to address that in a very practical way. She began to finish work at a certain time and not check e-mails during the evening. She did not turn the TV on every evening so that she could have more social interaction with the family and she arranged to go out to dinner once a month with her husband.

The influential people that we have observed know their values and keep them at the front of their mind constantly. They will also talk about what they value in a way that helps others to understand their position.

Exercise: Defining your values

Make a list of the 10 values which you feel are most important to you. My top ten values are:

1 ....
2 ....
3 ....
4 ....
5 ....
6 ....
7 ....
8 ....
9 ....
10 ....

Example:

This example was written by a manager attending a course on leadership:

Value: Personal Development

What personal development means to me

Development has always been both a value and a passion for me. I have always sought out opportunities to learn new things, take up new challenges and use the value I place on learning as a foundation for both my personal and professional development. Learning also excites and inspires me and is a source of energy.

How much I connect with it in my daily life

As a leader I have always shared this value with my team and colleagues and constantly encourage them to take up development opportunities. This was all well and good, but around 6 months ago I realized that over the last 12-18 months I had participated in no new learning experiences. I had read no new books, attended no courses or conferences, done no new research or led no new projects.

I had been a learning free zone!

I realized that the demands of both work and home had been such that very subtly I had lost touch with one of the most important values in my life and work. Both from a personal point of view and as a role model to my staff I felt this was really unacceptable.

Having made the realization, the first thing I did was sit down and look at what type of development I felt I needed at this stage and came up with 2 areas :

Refreshing my leadership development, I wanted to see what new things were out there for leaders and access some form of leadership development which was group based in the next 6 months.

Reading material: I love books and at one of the last conferences I did attend I heard Deepak Chopra speak and was inspired by some of the concepts he was looking at – I decided to order 2 of his books as a starting point of getting back to reading.

Now having read this example have a go with just 2 of your values. Identify the 2 values which you hold most dear and (on the next page) under each one write a paragraph about what this value means to you and how much you feel you connect with it in your daily life.

What the value .... means to me is:

....

....

....

....

How much I connect with it in my daily life is:

....

....

....

....

2 actions I will take in connection with this value are:

....

....

What the value .... means to me is:

....

....

....

....

How much I connect with it in my daily life is:

....

....

....

....

2 actions I will take in connection with this value are:

....

....

Case Study

A delegate on one of our training programmes used this exercise on her values in the following way.

I realized that I had a very strong value around collaboration and working together and although I believed in these values, they had become subsumed in my working life because everyone in my team (including me), felt overworked and stretched on a daily basis. We were all so focused on our own work that we rarely lifted our heads up to check on colleagues, ask for help and share ideas. People would constantly say things like, "just let me get to the end of the week." "I can't think about that now, I have to get this done by lunchtime." "Lunchtime – what's that?" We only ever talked to complain about workload or throw out slightly bitter lines like the ones above. I was just as bad as everyone else. When I came on your course and we did the exercise on values, I decided that I wanted to start working more collaboratively, sharing work and helping other people in my team. My motivation was quite simply I was sick of being miserable at work! I hoped that if I started to model these values then other people would follow my example and we could all be a bit happier.

I decided that the following day, I would go into work and do 2 things:

✓ Allocate 20 minutes in the morning and 20 minutes in the afternoon in which I would do something to help a colleague. I felt that 40 minutes away from my own tasks would neither make nor break the week!

✓ Ask our administrator to reinstate team meetings. We used to hold these fortnightly but stopped having them because we were all too busy.

The day started well, I looked at my work and decided to allocate my first 20 minutes at 11.00am. I stopped work at 11, stood up and said pretty loudly, "I have 20 minutes to spare, can I do anything for anyone?" The shock was quite funny really, everyone just stared at me. A couple of people muttered something like, "wish I had 20 minutes to spare – lucky you."

I was a bit intimidated but I continued to look round and said, "seriously, can I do anything for anyone?" One colleague said rather tentatively, "Could you just copy these for me?", and held out some reports – she then said, "I mean if you are sure." I said, "I wouldn't have offered if I didn't mean it," took the reports and went and copied them.

When I came back into the office, my colleague thanked me and said "That was good of you." I took a deep breath and said, "Well something we did yesterday made me think that if we all used a bit of our time to help each other we may find that we can make things a bit easier. I've also asked if we can have the team meetings back. I just think we've stopped working together and we should start again, at least in small ways, if we can." A few more people were listening and a couple of people said they thought I was right and they would like to get the team meetings back.

The upshot that day was that we spent around half an hour talking about how we could work a bit better together and something's started to change. I'm not saying it was all perfect at once because it wasn't but we have continued and people are very used to "the 20 minute help out" now which is what we have called it. I really felt I influenced my team to work differently.

Once you start to connect more strongly to your values and act on them, you are behaving authentically – this generates trust and trust is a key component of influence.

Intent

Another cornerstone of our trustworthiness is to have good intent. This is about genuinely being as concerned about the other person as we are about ourselves. It is about having a clear and open agenda and ensuring that our actions and decisions are motivated by mutually serving rather than self-serving motives.

"The moment there is suspicion about a person's motives, everything they do becomes tainted." Mahatma Ghandi

What do you believe the intent is when you hear the following?

➢ "I hear what you are saying."

➢ "With all due respect I think you will find...."

➢ "I don't want to disagree with you I am just playing devil's advocate."

It is rare that people believe the words in these phrases – the usual reaction is that the speaker's real intent is to undermine or manipulate. As soon as that happens our ability to influence in that situation is diminished

Behaviors that generate trust

So how does this translate into practise, what makes us trust some people and not others?

Exercise: Behaviors that generate trust

Identify 5 people that you know and write their names down

e.g. manager, colleague, relative, friend, member of staff

Try to think of some people that you do trust and some that you do not.

1 ....
2 ....
3 ....
4 ....
5 ....

Think about the people you have identified and the general patterns of behavior that you experience from them. Now generate two lists – those behaviors that encourage trust in the people you have identified and a second list of those behaviors that discourage trust.

Behaviors that discourage trust:

Behaviors that encourage trust:

Having run this exercise many times over the years the following are typical examples of behaviors that people identify.

Behaviors that discourage trust:

- ✘ Saying different things to different people
- ✘ Failing to keep promises
- ✘ Not sharing feelings
- ✘ Blaming others
- ✘ Scapegoating others
- ✘ Manipulation
- ✘ Saying one thing and doing another
- ✘ Talking about people behind their backs
- ✘ Dishonesty
- ✘ Hiding or not sharing information
- ✘ Betraying confidences
- ✘ Never asking for help

Behaviors that encourage trust:

- ✓ Being willing and able to listen without judging
- ✓ Making time for people
- ✓ Openness
- ✓ Sharing information willingly
- ✓ Doing things without expecting anything in return
- ✓ Showing compassion
- ✓ Honesty
- ✓ Demonstrates integrity
- ✓ Practicing what you preach
- ✓ Being pleased for people when things go well for them
- ✓ Giving positive feedback
- ✓ Having the difficult conversations when they are necessary
- ✓ Displaying sincerity
- ✓ Clear communication
- ✓ Being clear about your expectations of others
- ✓ Trusting others

Review the list above and consider which you display – this may be difficult to assess yourself and you may need to seek feedback from others.

Developing your trustworthiness

All the things that have been discussed so far in this chapter rely on people knowing you well enough to trust you. A key area we can therefore work on in becoming more influential is building and developing strong relationships.

Exercise: Building relationships

Charting your network

1. Draw a picture of yourself or write your name in the middle of the following page.
2. Identify all the people in your life that you communicate with regularly and therefore sometimes need to influence – put these names on the chart.
3. Consider how strong each relationship is - if the relationship is very strong draw a thick line between you and that person, if it is non existent do not draw a line and if it is weak draw a dotted line.

Example:

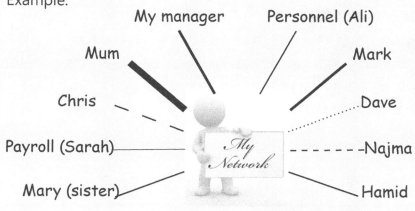

Chart your network:

Look at your network and consider the following questions:

Are there areas that need to be strengthened?

Do you invest a lot of time in some areas of your network and not enough in others?

Identify someone in your network that you feel you need to develop a more trusting relationship with.

What do you think are the reasons for the lack of trust?

Look back at the list of behaviors that generate trust and identify three things that you can do to build trust with that person.

1 ....

2 ....

3 ....

Summary of Trait 3: Trustworthiness

In summary to develop this trait, concentrate on:

✓ Being clear about what your values are and what they mean

✓ Ensuring that you are being consistent with those values and therefore behaving authentically

✓ Checking that when you are dealing with people that you are open and honest and that your intent is good – in other words you are genuinely concerned about the other person as well as yourself

✓ Exhibiting the behaviors in your everyday life that generate trust and avoiding the ones that discourage it

✓ Investing time and energy in building relationships with people

Further Reading:

Liberating the Corporate Soul, Richard Barrett, Butterworth-Heineman, 978-0750670715

The Speed of Trust (The One Thing That Changes Everything), Stephen R Covey and Rebecca Merrill, Simon and Schuster, 978-0743295604

www.valuescentre.com

Trait 4:
Empathy

"If you learn just a single trick, Scout,
you'll get along a lot better with all kinds of folks.
You never really understand a person until you consider
things from his point of view ...
until you climb inside of his skin and walk around in it."

Atticus Finch

Trait 4:
Empathy

In this section, we will be:

✓ Defining empathy

✓ Explaining the importance of exploring other people's points of view

✓ Discussing the key skills of empathizing i.e. insightful questioning and active listening

✓ Providing guidance on how to develop your ability to empathize

"People will forget what you said, people will forget what you did, but people will never forget how you made them feel."
Bonnie Jean Wasmund

What is empathy?

Empathy is the capability to share and understand another's emotion and feelings. It is often characterized as the ability to "put oneself into another's shoes," or in some way experience what the other person is feeling.

So how does experiencing what another person is feeling help us become more influential?

If someone makes us feel:

➢ Understood

➢ Listened to

➢ Respected

➢ Intelligent

➢ Appreciated

➢ Valued or

➢ Trusted

then we will want to reciprocate and will therefore become open to helping them feel the same way.

People who we feel understand us are the people we are open to being influenced by. There is often a myth that empathic people are from the "soft and fluffy" school of thought. Nothing could be further from the truth. Empathic people succeed in life BECAUSE they can influence and collaborate successfully with other people.

When people talk about becoming more influential they often think about impressing their point on others. Influential people understand that to influence anyone we have to be able to understand their view of the world. They get the other point of view and work with what others think, feel and believe.

Maps of the world – exploring other points of view

Consider the above image. We often sit on top of our own mountain and focus only on the view from there. This is the view which is often described as our map of the world and is formulated from our own perspective and experience. In order to influence we have to be prepared to climb down our own mountain and get onto the top of someone else's mountain to see the world from their perspective.

I love this metaphor because in addition to making the point about seeing the world differently it also gives a sense of effort. Empathy and really understanding others does take effort. Naturally, we can much more easily see our own perspective simply because it is our own and to then put that perspective on one side in order to truly look at someone else's is quite a stretch. However, the bottom line is that we will never become influential without being prepared to do this.

When people ask for better communication they are asking for better understanding, so when we are able to make others feel understood – we really do start to implant a feeling which stays with others for a long time and will inevitably increase our influence with them.

Many people come to training and coaching sessions wanting to change a perspective in someone else. Nine times out of ten, they will only be looking at the situation from their own map of the world.

Case Study

Recently this situation was raised by a coachee. He managed in a customer service environment where many of the customers had difficulty accessing their services between 9-5. There was already some flexible opening which included opening at 8.30 am and one night a week staying open until 7 pm. It was proposed that these opening times should be increased to opening at 8 am and staying open 4 nights a week until 7 pm. This meant that the working patterns of the staff had to be changed and this was causing a lot of problems. There had already been one staff meeting which was very turbulent and no agreement had been reached.

The coachee came to the session angry and frustrated. His view was that his staff were being short sighted and stubborn. If they did not extend opening hours then business would decline and this could cause a threat to jobs. The coachee could not understand why his staff could not see this. His approach was that he was not going to talk any more – he would just bring the new system in and people would have to lump it. He was worried however, as he knew that this would not give him staff really focused on helping customers and that also would affect business.

In the session we started by looking at the situation from his staffs perspective. We talked around their motivations for the job, family problems this might cause i.e. childcare, partners work patterns and also social engagements. As we talked more about the fact that these were issues, the manager softened and started talking about how he would also be affected by these things and that he did understand how his staff felt. He ended by saying "They probably see me as a cold hearted b.......... who doesn't care at all about their lives but only cares about the bottom line – that isn't going to make them want to work on a solution with me is it?"

BINGO!

This was not just about the actual resistance to the change in working patterns this was resistance to him and the staff's perception that he neither valued or appreciated their views and problems.

It is such a common mistake from managers, they really do not see how their lack of empathy raises not just resistance to a situation but direct resistance to them. Capacity to influence plummets!

This particular manager changed his approach completely. He went to see all of his staff on a one to one basis, apologized for his previous attitude and talked to them about all their individual views. He then called another meeting in which he fed back what he had learned and invited their input into how they implemented the new hours. It turned out the staff did see the need and now they felt understood and valued, they wanted to get involved in solving the problem. Rotas were worked out to suit people's individual needs as far as possible and shifts that caused real problems could be kept to a minimum e.g. a woman whose childcare had been an issue was, with the co-operation of her colleagues, able to structure most of her shifts to coincide with her husbands work patterns. It only meant her paying for 2 extra childcare sessions per month which she was happy with.

This meant that the new system was brought in under a spirit of co-operation not conflict.

The manager's empathy won through – he influenced successfully to the end he wanted, with much less pain!

The skills of empathizing – insightful questioning and active listening

The key skills we use when exploring someone else's map of the world are insightful questioning and active listening. These are also clearly skills of a strong communication capability which is discussed in Trait 6, however, because they are core to empathy we felt it was appropriate to cover them in this chapter.

Insightful questioning

What do we mean by insightful questioning?

The kind of questions that create dialogue and help to draw people out so that you can really understand their point of view are the kind of questions we are talking about here.

These are primarily open questions, those which open up a conversation by prompting a more detailed answer rather than those which just invite a yes or no response. They are used to prompt both yourself and the other person to deeper insights.

Open questions allow the speaker to help you understand their viewpoint. Closed questions can only give you information.
A closed question has a right or wrong (and often short) answer.
E.g. How many reams of paper are left? Where is the report? Did you find the room?

Some useful open questions to help foster empathic conversations are:

➢ "Tell me more about..............."

➢ "Can you give me an example?"

➢ "I hadn't thought of it in that way please could you give me more detail?"

➢ "Can you help me to understand your viewpoint?"

➢ "How is that affecting you?"

➢ "What do you want to happen?"

➢ "How would you like to see this develop from here?"

➢ "What stops you from............... ?"

➢ "What are the results you want?"

➢ "What outcome would you choose?"

➢ "What are your thoughts about .... ?"

➢ "How can I support you with this?"

Active listening

What do we mean by active listening?

Active listening is an intent to listen for meaning as well as for words. This means paying attention to the feeling behind the words and expressing understanding of the meaning the person wants to convey.

> **Exercise: Barriers to listening**
>
> Think about the last time you were trying to listen to someone and you found it difficult – what were the main reasons that you struggled to listen properly?
>
> ....
> ....
> ....
> ....

Some common reasons for switching off are:

- ✗ Being biased about either the person or the topic and therefore deciding that it is not worth listening.

- ✗ Formulating our own argument. This is such a common mistake when we passionately want to influence a situation. We are listening only for cues that will allow us to jump in with our next point.

- ✗ Becoming distracted by other things that are going on around us.

- ✗ Becoming distracted by things that we are thinking.

- ✗ Drifting off because what we are hearing is too complicated or complex.

- ✗ Deciding that we already know what someone is going to say and therefore there is no need to listen.

You may have listed others and it is important to recognize how hard it is to listen well – our average listening span is about 7 minutes and so it is something that we do have to work at.

Think about the barriers that you identified in that exercise and decide to consciously start to practice stopping yourself doing those things in your next conversation.

Influential people work very hard at both their questioning and listening skills and using these skills artfully is one of the most respectful and empathic things you can do for anyone.

Active listening is completely different in its quality from auto pilot listening. It is a structured way of listening and responding to others – it focuses attention on the speaker. If we do not make a conscious effort to do this we often hijack the conversation very quickly. Usually this hijack occurs within the first minute of a conversation and happens when we start to talk about our own experiences or begin to give advice. Suspending our judgement in order to fully attend to the other person immediately increases our ability to understand and therefore influence.

Aspects of active listening include:

✓ Looking at the person, and suspending other things you are doing and thinking about.

✓ Listening not merely to the words, but the feelings behind the words.

✓ Becoming aware of the things which can stop you listening – we can all switch off for various reasons and it is important to recognize that whenever this happens you are not really listening.

✓ Using verbal reinforcers such as "I see" and "yes" when appropriate.

✓ Avoiding distracting behaviors such as fidgeting.

✓ Seeking clarification if the meaning is not clear.

✓ Minimizing interruptions.

Developing your empathy

The following couple of exercises give you a structured approach to seeing others perspectives.

Exercise: Image exchange

Think of a person or group that you have difficulty empathizing with. This exercise is a useful way to try and understand the other person's point of view. Write down your side of the story and then try and think what the other person's side of the story might be

My side of the story is:

....

....

....

I think ....'s side of the story is:

....

....

....

What might you need to do to empathize with them more?

....

....

....

Exercise: Alternative viewpoints

This exercise can be used on your own or with a team when trying to look at an issue from a number of different viewpoints. Place the issue in the center of a piece of paper. Write all the names of people or groups who may have a view about that issue around the outside. Work round the stakeholders offering ideas about what you think that person or groups perspective on the issue would be.

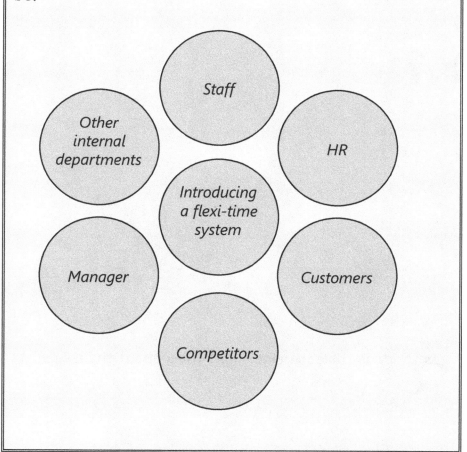

Draw your own diagram about an issue that is relevant to you.

List 5 ideas someone else might think about the issue:

1

2

3

4

5

Summary of trait 4:
Empathy

In summary, to develop this trait concentrate on:

- ✓ Getting off your own mountain and climbing up the other mountain! Make the effort!
- ✓ Using insightful questions and active listening
- ✓ Develop your ability to see others perspectives by using structured exercises

Further Reading:

The Seven Habits of Highly Effective People, Stephen R Covey, Simon and Schuster, 978-0684858395

NLP at Work, Sue Knight, Nicholas Brealey, 978-1857883022

Social Intelligence, Daniel Goleman, Arrow Books, 978-0099464921

www.danielgoleman.info

www.businessballs.com/empathy.htm

Trait 5:
Inspirational

"There are those who look at things the way they are, and ask why ...
I dream of things that never were, and ask why not?"

Robert Francis Kennedy

Trait 5:
Inspirational

In this section we will be:

✓ Clarifying why the ability to inspire is part of influencing

✓ Defining what being inspirational really means

✓ Developing your ability to inspire yourself and tap into your power to inspire

✓ Providing guidance on how to develop the skill of enthusing and inspiring others

"Remember if you want to become an inspiration to others, you must first become an inspiration to yourself." Gareth Brown.

What do we mean by inspirational?

The next trait which influential people demonstrate is that of inspiration.

Few people would question how important the ability to inspire is to influencing and yet many people will flinch at the idea of inspiring others. We turn away from our own ability to do that, thinking that the ability to inspire is granted only to a few – those special charismatic ones in the world.

Yet, when we ask people who has inspired them, most people speak of someone they know, often a parent, a teacher, sometimes someone they have worked with or for. This indicates that we all have the power to inspire.

It is crucial to your influencing power that you believe that you hold the power to inspire others. As we unpick inspiration, keep that thought in the forefront of your mind.

So, what is inspiration? The dictionary definitions are:

"Arousal of the mind to special or unusual activity or creativity;

a product of your creative thinking and work;

a sudden intuition as part of solving a problem or

stirring to a particular emotion or action."

Inspiration therefore, is what moves us, what stimulates us what creates our capacity for action. We believe that this is a particularly useful way of thinking about inspiration and if you think of those definitions most of us will be able to fairly easily identify occasions when we have inspired ourselves.

We have perhaps been inspired when:

- ✓ We have produced something out of our own creative thinking.
- ✓ Had moments when we felt stimulated by an exciting idea to special or unusual activity or creativity.
- ✓ Had a flash of insight which helped us to solve a problem or felt stirred into action.

These moments are the first steps to becoming an inspiration to ourselves.

Inspiring yourself

Influential people not only make the most of such moments but they work at creating more inspiration within their own lives and thereby inspire others to do the same. Influential people inspire in us not just a belief in them but in ourselves.

"I'm asking you to believe. Not just in my ability to bring about real change in Washington. I'm asking you to believe in yours."
Barack Obama

Influential people also radiate enthusiasm. If you feel inspired yourself, then it is easier to feel and project enthusiasm, however, influential people can be roused to enthusiasm simply by another's great idea. We often hear people say that they sometimes lose touch with their own inspiration and don't feel they are inspired "enough", but they can still feel enthused to encourage someone else's idea and therefore, start to feel more inspired themselves. Whether your inspiration comes from creating inspiring moments for yourself or by inspiring others – it still taps into your creativity and strengthens your influencing capacity.

The key is to recognize how you become inspired.

WE ALL HAVE THE POWER TO INSPIRE

Elements of being inspirational are:

✓ Inspiring and motivating yourself

✓ Creating inspired action

✓ Encouraging others to get inspired

As we connect with our ability to inspire, we express qualities of enthusiasm, excitement and confidence. We are able then to pass this onto others because we believe it. Action is also a part of this - taking action in itself is inspirational. Influential people act. They do not allow their fears to hold them back, they move forward and do something rather than nothing.

The following exercises are designed to help you increase your ability to inspire and motivate yourself, create inspired action and encourage others to get inspired.

Exercise: Inspirational moments and inspirational action

This exercise is designed to help you think through your own inspirational moments and what actions you are creating as a result.

Consider those dictionary definitions again:-

"Arousal of the mind to special or unusual activity or creativity; a product of your creative thinking and work; a sudden intuition as part of solving a problem or stirring to a particular emotion or action."

Identify any occasions in the last 6 months when you have been stimulated by an exciting idea or thought into unusual:

➢ activity or creativity
➢ or produced something creative
➢ or had an intuition/sudden idea/change of perspective which has helped you solve a problem
➢ or been emotionally stirred into action

Please list any occasions which fall into these categories on the following page. If at this stage, the list is quite short or even if you cannot think of anything, don't worry, the purpose of this is to simply identify if inspiration is a trait that you need to work on.

My inspirational moments in the last 6 months:

....

....

....

....

....

....

When you have completed your list, think about:

How easy was it to think of inspirational moments?

How many occasions did you identify? There is no rule about how many inspired thoughts and actions you can and should have, this is a simple check for you to decide if you are accessing your inspiration as much as you could.

What action followed on from your first inspiration?

What other ideas have been stimulated by this exercise?

....

....

....

....

....

....

....

One of the great things about thinking about inspiration is.....
you get more inspired!

Tips to increase your inspirational moments:

Think about your previous list, when you were creating inspired ideas and inspired actions :

➢ Were you alone or was someone with you?

➢ If there was someone with you, who was it and what was their contribution to your moment of inspiration?

➢ Where were you?

➢ Was there anything you were seeing, hearing, touching, smelling or tasting which contributed to your moment of inspiration?

➢ What was your state of mind at the time?

➢ How were you feeling physically?

➢ Did you do something specific to help your creativity? If so what was it?

The purpose of this reflection is to start your thinking process on how your moments of inspiration are created. Many people find that a particular place, person, view, smell, piece of music, poem etc. helps them to feel inspired and to create more inspiration in your life, you create circumstances which will assist that process.

Example:

These are some of things that people on our Beyond Imagination course have identified help when they need inspiration:

✓ Conversations with people who energise me
✓ Simon and Garfunkel's Bridge Over Troubled Water and Westlife's I Believe In Angels
✓ A photograph my husband took on a holiday to Bali which is of hundreds of water lilies bursting into bud, which I have in my office
✓ Water, the ocean, rivers, lakes
✓ Walking
✓ Swimming
✓ Inspirational quotes e.g. Don't Quit
✓ Sun (or pictures of sunny places)
✓ Pictures of my adopted Born Free Moon Bear Ginny
✓ Poetry, particularly the poem "The Journey" by Mary Oliver

If you can identify those things which help you feel inspired, you can develop ways of accessing them when you need inspiration.

Some suggestions for staying close to your inspiration are:

✓ Create a visualization board with pictures which inspire
✓ Keep quotations somewhere visible
✓ Sign up to a motivational website
✓ Keep audio tapes and CD's which inspire you in your car and listen to them often
✓ Buy inspirational books
✓ Practice meditating on the things which inspire you

If you stay connected to those things which inspire you, you will feel more energized and creative and this energy will help you to grow your ability to inspire others.

Exercise: Things that inspire me

List 3 things that inspire you:

1 ....
2 ....
3 ....

Inspiring others

*"Life doesn't require that we be the best,
only that we try our best."* H.Jackson Brown

You may think – what about those days when I feel as if my inspiration has gone, can I still be inspirational to others? Yes you can, because when it comes to inspiring others one thing stands out – enthusiasm! When we are enthusiastic and optimistic about someone's talents, ideas or qualities, we strike a chord which starts to help others to feel inspired. It is a lot easier, as we said before to radiate enthusiasm when you feel inspired but not impossible. Many people will know that even on a low day when your child, partner or colleague needs some active encouragement, you find it and by starting to express enthusiasm for their ideas, you automatically start to perk up and feel more inspired yourself.

Enthusing and inspiring others will always increase your energy and sense of inspiration. This is a virtuous circle and it doesn't matter whether on a particular day you start from feeling inspired yourself or by getting energized and enthused by someone else's idea it all increases your ability to become inspired and to inspire others. Enthusiasm is contagious in the most positive way.

One of the results of this contagion is that you will become someone who actively encourages ideas from other people and being an idea grower is one of the most powerful characteristics of influential people. An influential person is rarely precious about their own ideas, they will fully acknowledge how inspirational they find the ideas of others, and will openly express enthusiasm, praise and encouragement to others to both have ideas and to act on them. Thus, influential people help to grow inspiration in other people.

One of the enemies of inspiration is our inner critic which we refer to in the section on knowing what you want and believing you can achieve it (trait 1). Influential people increase their ability to inspire by both managing their own inner critic and helping others to manage their inner critic. One of the greatest deterrents to creativity is the inner voice that constantly whispers in our ear that we're not good enough, that nobody will approve of what we're doing and that they don't really like us anyway. No one other than yourself can do the work of eradicating the inner critic completely. However, it is possible to help others listen to their positive voice rather than their negative voice and therefore, help them to increase their creativity and inspiration. This is where influential people score – they help other people manage that inner critic and keep it in the right place.

Another powerful way to encourage others to become inspired is to stimulate their imagination and create situations and environments in which ideas can flourish. Pixar is a company known for innovation and creativity. Films such as Toy Story, The Incredibles and Wall.E have demonstrated that and yet unlike many other film studios all their stories, worlds and characters are created internally. Part of their ability to do this comes from consistently applying three operating principles:

- ✓ Everyone in the organization must have freedom to communicate with anyone.

- ✓ It must be safe for everyone to offer ideas.

- ✓ We must stay close to innovations that are happening in the academic community.

Tips for inspiring other people:

➤ Ask them what enthuses them and encourage them to talk about those things.

➤ Radiate enthusiasm.

➤ Praise people for new ideas and encourage them to develop their ideas further.

➤ Get comfortable with ambiguity.

➤ Encourage curiosity and questions, actively praise people for being curious.

➤ Use creative techniques such as imagery, metaphor, storytelling and encourage others to do the same.

➤ Provide opportunities for people to work in inspiring environments if possible, think about space, light, pictures, music, color, nature and bring them into your environment if possible.

➤ Allow ideas to incubate and reach maturity (both your own ideas and those of others).

Some of the above suggestions such as creative imagery may feel unfamiliar, however, they can be woven into all kinds of situations if you allow yourself some space to think slightly differently. The following example demonstrates this.

Case Study

We did this exercise in a workshop, in which one of the delegates wanted to find an inspirational image to use as part of a presentation to a group of her staff to explain how the service they were providing in the university was changing and would need to adapt to accommodate a wider cross section of students.

She came up with the idea of using a tea towel she had bought with a map of the London Underground on it. She started to describe how routes through the university were going to be like a train service. Traditionally students had got on the train at the start of a journey and stayed on it until the end. However there were now many more choices. Firstly people can choose which route they want to take (the qualification) and they can choose how long the journey is going to be (full time study, part time, distance learning etc). People can get off the train and break their journey for a few days or a year. The lines and routes on the map intersect and cross over which allows people to change course or direction fairly easily if they want to. As she continued with the analogy people became quite animated and started to describe ways that the service they offered would need to change to meet the changing environment. Her feedback was that the session went exceptionally well and the image prompted all kinds of ideas that no one had expressed before and really motivated the whole team.

This is a great example of how an influential person can use an inspirational image to encourage inspiration in others.

Exercise: Using creative imagery

Identify an individual or group that you would like to encourage to generate more ideas or actions.

Think of an image that you can present either verbally or visually that you believe will inspire them and help them access their creative imagination.

Write down a description of your image and also put in some kind of visual representation (this can be a drawing, photograph, collage etc.).

Identify who you will present it to and when.

Create Your Image:

Summary of trait 5:
Inspirational

In summary, to develop this trait concentrate on:

✓ Believing in your power to inspire

✓ Focusing on your inspirational moments

✓ Making time to connect with people and things which inspire you

✓ Being enthusiastic about other peoples ideas, talents and qualities

✓ Encouraging curiosity in yourself and others

✓ Praising others and actively ask for their ideas

✓ Capturing ideas which inspire, do not let them drift away

✓ Practicing developing creative images

✓ Acting on your inspiration!

Further Reading:

Thinkertoys - A Handbook of Business Creativity, Michael Michalko, Ten Speed Press, 978-1580087735

Boost Your Creative Intelligence, Harry Alder, Kogan Page, 978-0749437060

Creative Manager's Pocketbook, John Townsend and Jacques Favier, Management Pocketbooks, 978-1870471695

The Eighth Habit, Stephen R Covey, Simon and Schuster, 978-0743206839

www.positive-way.com

www.stephencovey.com

Trait 6:
Strong communication capability

"I am the most spontaneous speaker in the world
because every word, every gesture,
and every retort has been carefully rehearsed."

George Bernard Shaw

Trait 6:
Strong communication capability

In this section we will be:

✓ Defining strong communication capability

✓ Clarifying the elements of a strong communication capability

    ➢ Verbal impact

        ‣ The ability to structure verbal communication with clarity and logic;
        ‣ Contextualizing your language;
        ‣ Avoiding unhelpful language patterns;
        ‣ Ability to structure insightful questions and listen really well

    ➢ Non-verbal impact

        ‣ Voice projection and great use of emphasis and tone
        ‣ Image and personal presentation
        ‣ Congruence

✓ Written impact

✓ Impact in presentations

"Good communication is as stimulating as black coffee, and just as hard to sleep after." Anne Morrow Lindbergh

What is a strong communication capability?

*"The ability to communicate powerfully in
a range of ways and in a range of situations."*

Influential people are at ease with all the elements of a strong communication capability and able to express themselves using a variety of those elements as appropriate. This trait is the catalyst for using the other traits. We must be able to communicate our sense of purpose, our empathy, our expertise, our open-mindedness to others in order to influence them. Honing our communication capability is vital to increasing our influence.

As well as being skilled in all the elements of a strong communication capability, influential people are able to judge which method of communication is appropriate to particular situations. This is very important, a powerful message can be killed by the wrong method of communication and is immeasurably strengthened by the right method.

Daniel Goleman author of Emotional Intelligence speaks of rich and lean or thick and thin communication. Face to face conversation is rich communication, email is lean communication.

Misunderstandings are highly prevalent in lean communication. Influential people choose rich over lean communication whenever possible as you are always better able to influence if you are in a rich communication environment.

The elements of a strong communication capability

We have identified 4 main elements of a strong communication capability that are important for influential people to master:

1. Verbal impact

2. Non-verbal impact

3. Written impact

4. Impact in formal presentations

There are different aspects of these 4 main elements which we have also looked at within this section to help clarify how to develop your communication capability to its best effect.

Exercise:
What are your strengths in communicating with others?

Think of 3 of your most recent successful communications. What made them work?

Verbal impact

Verbal impact includes a number of different aspects:

- ✓ Structuring our verbal communication with clarity and logic
- ✓ Contextualizing our language for the situation
- ✓ Avoiding unhelpful language patterns
- ✓ Ability to structure insightful questions and listen exceptionally well

Exercise: Listen to the world's best speakers

There are a lot of famous speakers who by the power of how they spoke and what they said changed history.

Have a listen to the following with your eyes closed:

I have a dream, Martin Luther King,
http://www.youtube.com/watch?v=PbUtL_0vAJk

Britian's finest hour, Winston Churchill
http://www.youtube.com/watch?v=LsKDGM5KTBY

One World, Mahatma Gandhi
http://www.youtube.com/watch?v=dk_RtLayZqY

Ability to structure our verbal communication with clarity and logic.

Many people lose their power to influence because of an inability to structure their conversations. It is really important to check on the logic and flow of your verbal communication. Waffling and rambling are not traits of influential people.

One of the reasons that logic and flow can get lost in verbal communication is that few people actually plan important conversations. We tend to plan written conversation in a much more structured way than we do verbal. Influential people plan their important verbal communication in as much detail as they do their written. Many situations in which you need to influence hang on a particular conversation, be that one on one or in a group or meeting situation. These conversations need to be planned carefully if you are to make them as influential/effective as possible.

If this is an important conversation and you want it to be an influential conversation, it deserves time and effort in preparation. Influential people prepare for important conversations!

Planning important conversations does not mean that you have to lose all spontaneity. There is real joy and power in those conversations that start at one point and then range into unexpected areas resulting in great ideas and new thinking. Some people believe that if they start to plan for the important conversations in their life then they will lose that spontaneity and willingness to allow new thinking to emerge. This is not so. Our experience shows that paradoxically, a plan gives you the confidence and ability to open yourself to new thinking and new ideas because you have a focus and this lessens your anxiety. You know that wherever the conversation goes, you can bring it back if you need to and allow it to develop further if you want to. Structure and planning are not the enemy of spontaneity.

Tips to help you structure your verbal communication:

When planning an important conversation or delivering an important message think about the following:

✓ What do I hope this conversation will achieve?

✓ What might the other person/people be thinking about the situation?/ What is their map of the world?

✓ What might they want to achieve?

✓ What are my concerns?

✓ What may their concerns be?

✓ How could we manage our mutual concerns?

✓ Am I making any assumptions, if so what are they?

✓ What is the checklist of things we need to discuss?

✓ What is the right time and place to have this conversation?

✓ Write a plan which covers all the above points. (This is not in order to read from a script but to clarify your thinking beforehand, reading from a script or plan would lessen your ability to influence rather than increase it.)

✓ Rehearse, with someone you trust who can give you feedback or at least rehearse out loud by yourself. Speaking aloud is very different from running something through in your mind. You will "hear" different things.

✓ Review your plan after practice and change it if need be.

✓ Practice again!

✓ Make sure that you practice enough so that your plan is firmly in your mind as you enter the conversation.

Contextualizing your language

A second element of powerful verbal communication is the ability to use language which is appropriate to the context. Influential people understand the importance of contextualizing their language to the situation and the person or people they are trying to influence.

There are a number of aspects to consider when choosing the right kind of language to use. For instance, if you want to inspire as part of your influencing then you need to choose language which is impactful and rich. Many highly influential figures are skilled in the use of rich language, creative imagery, metaphor and storytelling.

Consider Martin Luther King's "I have a dream" speech. His words have been repeated and replayed time and time again and their power is still as fresh and inspirational today as when he first gave the speech. Think of the following phrase

"Now is the time to lift our nation from the quicksands of racial injustice to the solid rock of brotherhood." Martin Luther King

The picture painted and the feelings that it evokes capture the imagination. In that context a factual account of racial injustice would not have been nearly as influential.

If however, you are facing a group of engineers who you wish to influence to use a particular piece of equipment or work a particular site, creative imagery is unlikely to be as impactful and may indeed be seen as fanciful or trite. Factual language, clarity and plain English will serve you much better.

Influencing a group of youths in a deprived area of an inner city to take part in community activity may require you to use informal language in order to have a conversation which they will find meaningful. Formal business language would be useless.

Influential people understand the concept of contextualizing their language to the situation in order to increase their influence.

Many people are only at ease using a particular form of language and within many organizations today business speak or management speak both obscures meaning and dumbs down the vocabulary. Influential people can say what they mean, have a wide vocabulary and tailor their language to the context.

Tips to help you develop the ability to contextualize your language:

✓ Widen your vocabulary by consciously using tools such as a Thesaurus and practicing using different words to express your meaning.

✓ Study plain English and avoid jargon and over complicated language.

✓ Practice thinking of and describing imaginative images with exercises such as the one in the chapter on inspiration.

✓ Write down a list of metaphors which appeal to you and start to include these in your conversations when appropriate.

✓ Familiarize yourself with the type of language used by different types of groups and individuals. Practice using different types of language in different contexts.

Avoiding unhelpful language patterns

Following on from the topic of contextualizing your language it is also worth looking at any language patterns you habitually use. We develop not just our vocabulary over time but also our patterns of language and there are several language patterns that should be avoided or at least used sparingly particularly when we are trying to influence others.

These include:

- ✗ **The exaggerated** – words such as always, never, everybody, all, often limit the scope for conversation – only use these when it is true!

- ✗ **The forcing** – telling people that they must, should or ought to do something usually produces a defensive /antagonistic response.

- ✗ **The definitive** – this language pattern involves making opinions sound like facts. It is the fine distinction between, "this is the only way to do the job" and "I believe this is the right way to do the job". The first statement discourages discussion where the second one leaves the door open for debate.

- ✗ **Deletions** – these are examples of language where parts of the meaning have been omitted. This is where "they" come into their own, "they wouldn't let us do that here". This language pattern implies that the speaker has no influence over what is happening around them.

- ✗ **Cliches** – these are expressions or phrases that have become trite through overuse. Clichés can sound both boring and patronizing if we are not careful. (Think of Ricky Gervais in the TV series The Office!) They are thought of as clichéd because they have been overused, so can also give the impression of lazy thinking. They are best avoided.

Tips to avoid unhelpful language patterns:

✓ Become aware of your language patterns and check yourself to see if you are using or overusing any of the above. Although it makes many people cringe initially, having a tape or video of yourself is incredibly helpful to study both your voice and your language patterns. Many courses on voice will offer this service.

✓ Get feedback if possible, a discussion on unhelpful language patterns with a trusted group of colleagues and friends can generate helpful feedback on any patterns you may be unaware of.

Ability to structure insightful questions and to listen really well

We have already dealt with skilful questioning and active listening in the chapter on empathy, however, it is such an important part of strong communication capability that it is worth reinforcing again.

Our verbal impact is not just about our ability to deliver our own messages. The way we question and listen to others is a very large part of the impact of our verbal communication. Insightful questioning is highly influential. David Taylor, the author of The Naked Leader talks of a meeting about a new project in which all he did was repeat over and over again, "How does this discussion move us forward?" He says that, people still talk of his contribution to the success of that project although it was several years ago.

Listening really well to someone is also highly influential. As we spoke about in the chapter on empathy someone who listens to us and makes us feel understood is someone we will be prepared to listen to in return. Influential people understand the power of skilful questions and are excellent listeners.

Tips to increase your questioning and listening ability

✓ Seek out exercises on questioning and listening. There are lots which can be accessed on the internet by Googling communication skills or questioning and listening. We have provided a couple in the chapter on empathy.

✓ Write a list of useful questions which you could use in a variety of situations. Just writing the list will help to embed these in your mind.

✓ Always be aware of when you are listening and when you are not listening. Make a conscious effort to bring yourself back whenever you switch off.

Non-verbal impact

Much has been written about non-verbal impact and its importance to how we are perceived. Impressions are based upon instinct and emotion, not on rational thought or in-depth investigation. They are the products of the associations we make between outward characteristics and the inner qualities we believe they reflect. Many of these outward characteristics are non-verbal.

Therefore to increase your influence it is vital that you pay as much attention to your non-verbal impact as that of your verbal impact. We are going to look at several areas of non-verbal impact which we believe are key to honing your communication capability.

These include:

- ✓ Voice projection
- ✓ Use of emphasis and tone
- ✓ Image and personal presentation
- ✓ Congruence

Voice projection and great use of emphasis and tone

Influential people are aware of the quality of their voice. It sounds obvious but volume and projection of voice have a big impact on how influential we can be.

Flat tones and lack of emphasis are blocks to people receiving the impact of what we have to say. Training the voice is not just for professional presenters and singers. Often we can correct problems such as speaking too quietly, varying our tone, speaking too quickly and use of emphasis, ourselves once we are aware of them. As mentioned earlier, getting yourself taped or videoed in order to listen to how your voice sounds to others is a really useful thing to do, in order to become aware of any problems. Voice coaching is another option to help you make the most of your voice and many influential people in public life do get help with their voice.

Understanding the power of your voice and taking measures to maximize it to best effect can strongly increase your communication capability.

Tips to maximize the power of your voice:

✓ Get a tape or video of yourself in order to become aware of how your voice sounds to others.

✓ Decide on anything you need to correct and practice speaking more slowly, varying your tones etc.

✓ Get feedback from others on how you sound.

✓ Think about accessing voice coaching.

Image and personal presentation

Image is a controversial topic but in our opinion it does matter! The key is the balance between matching your image and personal presentation to the context in which you wish to influence and also having a personal image which says the things you want to say about you. Highly influential people do pay attention to their image and personal presentation. By this we do not always mean presenting yourself "suited and booted". We do mean making sure your image and personal presentation reflects the side of yourself you really want to show.

It has long been asserted that we make up our minds about people we meet for the first time within two minutes – indeed some research shows that it takes as little as thirty seconds, and some of the latest thinking puts it as two seconds!

The jury is still out on the exact length of time, however whether you take the maximum two minutes or the minimum two seconds, what this very clearly shows is that we make extremely swift decisions about people when we meet them for the first time. Most of us are aware of this on a subconscious if not a conscious level and are also open to changing our minds if and when we get to know people better. How many times have you said or had said to you, "you are nothing like I thought you were when we first met."

Preparing ourselves in terms of the personal impact we will make in those first vital minutes can set the tone of any relationship and give you the opportunity to build from the right place.

Case Study

Working with a group on personal presentation, one member of the group was a children and young peoples' worker and was involved in involving children in outdoor and leisure activities. She was concerned because she had been invited to speak at a conference and wanted to appear authentic, yet have credibility with the audience. She felt that buying a suit for the occasion would be entirely inappropriate, as she would be very uncomfortable – yet she hesitated to appear in her usual work clothes of jeans and t-shirt. We discussed how she could approach this and decided that she needed to take her image up one notch to give her a boost, but not try to be something she was not. Smart trousers, blouse and boots worked for her – she felt and looked right. A business suit would have totally worked against her. Again, if she was going to speak to a community group then jeans and t-shirt would be entirely right as it would give the image she wanted to present.

Tips to develop your image and personal presentation:

✓ Pay attention to your image – it sounds obvious but many people do not.

✓ Remember being casual is not the same as being untidy and badly groomed.

✓ Get help if you need it – image consultancies abound or just use a friend whose sense of style you admire.

✓ Present the image you want to present – make it appropriate to the situation.

Congruence

What do we mean by congruence? It is a Latin word that means to come together, to agree. In the context we are discussing congruence refers to our ability to deliver a congruent message, a clear single message as opposed to a mixed message. The process of giving a mixed message is sometimes referred to as "leakage" – we leak non-verbally what we are actually thinking! Incongruence is noticeable. We can see from non-verbal signals such as lack of eye contact, awkward gestures etc., when someone is saying something that they are clearly not comfortable about. This makes other people feel uncomfortable as we do not know which bit of the message to respond to – do we accept what is being said or follow our much stronger impression that it is not meant?

Our non-verbal impact needs to match our verbal impact for our message to be perceived as congruent. Face to face communication is made up of three things:

➢ The words we use

➢ The way we say them – tone, pitch, emphasis, volume etc.

➢ The body language we exhibit

When we are congruent these three elements are matched. When they are saying the same thing then 99% of the impact comes from the words. However, when the words, tone and body language do not match then only 7% of the impact comes from the words and 93% from the way they are delivered. This means that all your work on verbal impact can be ruined if your voice and body language which make up your non-verbal impact are incongruent.

As it says in the song, "it ain't what you do, it's the way that you do it…."

Imagine the following conversations:

Person 1 asked, *"Is anything wrong?"*

Person 2 looked like this

and replied, *"Nothing,"* with a hesitant voice.

Person 1 said, *"Sorry I am late."*

Person 2 looked like this

He said *"It's OK we really appreciate you turning up at all."* in a voice that was heavily sarcastic with extra emphasis on the words *at all*.

In these examples do you think you would believe what was being **said**?

It is key to recognize how important this is when talking about communication capability.

We feel comfortable with people who behave congruently – we believe them and we believe their message. This inevitably leads to a stronger influencing capacity.

Tips to improve your congruence:

✓ Back to the idea of a video again! To really know how congruent your verbal and non-verbal communication is, you need to be able to see yourself. As with voice, many training providers on presentation skills or image will provide a videoing service and it is well worth investing in this.

✓ If the idea of a video is too excruciating, then try out in front of the mirror. Practice delivering an important message and watch yourself. This is less effective as you do not see as much but will still help.

✓ Get feedback – you could make this part of a group or team exercise. Everyone could practice delivering important messages and getting feedback on how congruent they appeared.

✓ This really is an area where you need external input, either as feedback or use of some tool to be able to watch yourself back. Preferably both!

Written impact

Increasing your influence means increasing your written impact as well as your verbal and non-verbal impact. Many people concentrate on one or the other but to become more influential it is very important to cover both. There are a number of aspects to written communication including: constructing reports, writing letters, email protocol, PowerPoint presentations, articles and books. The wider our range of written communication skills, the more influential we can be on paper or screen as well as in person.

It is easier to misunderstand written communication than verbal because of the issue of rich and lean communication methods referred to at the beginning of the chapter. Written communication is leaner than verbal therefore, it is easier to misinterpret. You need to consider both potential for misunderstanding and misinterpretation.

Examples of written howlers:

From letters to councils:
"Our lavatory seat is broken in half and now it is in three pieces."
"Our kitchen floor is damp. We have two children and would like a third so will you please send someone around to do something about it."

From minutes of a meeting:
"I have discussed the issue of filling the stationery cupboard with my colleagues."

From student essays:
"Control of infectious diseases is very important in case an academic breaks out."

Written howlers are funny to read but embarrassing for the person who has written them. Written communication is one of the most common ways people can damage OR maximize their credibility. Make sure your written communication positively helps you increase your influence.

Tips to develop your written impact:

✓ Review your written skills and decide which ones you want to improve.

✓ Look at taking training courses – there are many correspondence and online courses in written skills.

✓ Develop both creative and business writing skills. Don't restrict yourself to purely business writing skills – many business reports benefit from the judicious use of imagery, metaphor and anecdotes. A language has grown around business communications that often makes them way too bland to be influential. Learn both sides of writing and use both!

✓ Always proof read and get other people to check important pieces of written communication for mistakes or howlers.

Impact in presentations

Formal presentations are such a big part of business life today that we could not end communication capability without mentioning them. They play a key role in many situations in which we are trying to influence the outcome. Giving a short presentation forms part of a lot of job interviews, tendering processes and bids for funding.

Speaking in public is also a powerful way to build your reputation. Presenting draws on verbal, non-verbal and written impact so all the previous information is relevant, however, they also include specific use of technology and confidence in group situations.

Influential people develop their presenting skills usually by both taking presenting courses and by practice. The mindset of "I hate presentations" or "I can't do presentations" is not helpful. As we will discuss in flexible thinking it is possible to change a mindset and once you do, it is one of the easiest skills to get help with, as there are lots of great courses and books specifically on presenting really well.

Tips to develop your presentation skills

✓ Review your presentations and get feedback on how influential they are.

✓ Look for a good presentation skills course – even experienced presenters benefit from a refresher and feedback.

✓ Practice presenting in safe situations, then when you come to a really important situation it will feel easier.

✓ Effective presentations have a clear structure – a beginning, a middle and an end.

✓ Remember that the peak of concentration for most people is in the first few minutes of a presentation. It is therefore imperative that you start with something that captures the audience's attention. This could be an interesting statistic, a relevant quote, an anecdote or a story.

✓ Most presenters find the first few minutes are the most stressful part of a presentation. Ensure that you have scripted, learned and rehearsed the opening. This should include who you are, the structure of the presentation, the objectives and an attention grabber.

✓ Our average listening span is seven minutes so ensure your presentation is punctuated with visual aids and interaction.

✓ Remember to consider why the audience is there and keep relating the content of your presentation back to their needs.

✓ Don't let the presentation run out of steam at the end – have a clear summary and an impactful way to finish.

Summary of trait 6:
Strong communication capability

In summary, to develop this trait concentrate on:

✓ Your ability to be at ease with a variety of methods of communication

✓ Choosing the right method – remember rich and lean!

✓ Work with the tips on the different elements - communication is complex and you need to hone all of the parts

✓ Get help – there is so much available on communication skills

✓ Get feedback – communication is about mutual understanding and feedback on how your communication is received is the only true measure

Further Reading:

Persuasion – the art of influencing people, James Borg, Prentice Hall, 978-0273712992

Knockout Presentations, Diana DiRiesta, Chandler House Press, 978-1886284258

High Impact Presentations, Lee Bowman and Jackie Stewart, Bene Factum Publishing, 978-0952275459

Communicator's Pocketbook, Sean Misteil, 978-1870471411

www.ezinearticles.com

Trait 7:
Open-mindedness

"Renew thyself completely each day; do it again,
and again, and forever again."

Trait 7:
Open-mindedness

In this section we will be:

✓ Defining what being open-minded means

✓ Identifying some of the things that stop us from being open-minded

✓ Examining the effect of negative thinking

✓ Reviewing how habits form

✓ Identifying ways to develop more flexible thinking

✓ Looking at a structured way to help consider other views before reaching a conclusion (PACE technique)

✓ Exploring the importance of seeking feedback on our approach and impact

✓ Listing ways to solicit feedback from others

"An open mind leaves a chance for someone to drop a worthwhile thought in it."

What is open-mindedness?

In this book we have been talking about the traits of people who are truly influential not people who gain compliance from others through manipulation or force. There is one final trait that influential people share – a willingness to be influenced themselves. It is not enough just to understand the views of others as described in the section on empathy, we also need to be able to adapt, alter or develop our ideas as things change. Influential people do not have a fear of being influenced and this requires open-mindedness. This can be defined as ready to entertain new ideas; an open-minded curiosity or open-minded impartiality.

How open-minded are you?

Let's start by looking at how easy it is to see things differently. The following exercises require you to either think creatively or to find a way to see a different perspective. This is not a test, it is purely a starting point for you to ascertain if this is an area that you need to work on.

> **Exercise: How open-minded are you?**
>
> 1. Look at the following image – can you see at least two different perspectives?

2. When did you last change your mind after listening to someone else's point of view?

....

....

....

3. How readily do you check out your ideas by asking people to challenge them?

....

....

....

4. Have a look at the example below and then complete the next one.

Issue: How do we keep the floor clean?

Restatement 1: How can we prevent people walking on the floor in dirty shoes?

Restatement 2 How can we protect the floor so that it does not get dirty?

Restatement 3 How can we clean the floor in a more efficient way?

Think of three different ways to state the following issue.

Issue: How to make our meetings less boring?

1. ....

2. ....

3. ....

What gets in the way of being open-minded?

Negative thinking

One of the difficulties that research has shown is that when we are presented with a new idea or a challenge:

80% of our first thoughts are negative.

Think about it. That is not 80% of **all** our thoughts, for those of you who consider yourselves to be positive people, but 80% of our **first** thoughts. This is another hard premise for many people to accept. However, it is true that when first faced with a new idea it will probably throw up a whole host of negative thoughts. If we are not careful, those first thoughts can then taint our thinking process and we dive into a negative spiral. This often leads us to point out flaws in ideas rather than looking for anything that could be encouraged. As Peter Drucker has said, "The innovative company understands that innovation starts with an idea, and ideas are somewhat like babies – they are born small, immature and shapeless." Influential people recognize this and are very good at fostering ideas and suggestions even if they are not fully formed.

The tendency to focus on the negative is particularly true when we are facing an area which takes us outside our comfort zone and many situations in which we need to increase our influence do exactly that. The trick is to understand the process and get past those first negative thoughts by increasing our positive thoughts and creating a positive spiral. One way to do this is to tell yourself that you have to think of three positive things about a new idea before you have earned the right to criticize it.

To recognize the importance of this trait we only have to consider the other end of the spectrum. We have all experienced the person who delights in "playing devil's advocate" or uses sarcasm or patronizing behavior to dismiss someone else's idea. We also know how much that behavior reduces that person's ability to really influence us.

Habit

"The only difference between a rut and a grave is depth."

We all form habits and patterns in our behavior and in our relationships and sometimes these can make it difficult for us to imagine doing something in a different way. In Robert Winston's book and TV series about the human mind he used the analogy of a cornfield to describe how these patterns of behavior develop. If you walk through a cornfield for the first time your footprints will flatten the corn and leave a faint trail. When you come to walk through it again you will probably walk along the same path because it is easier. After the path has been trodden many times the passage through becomes very clear and easy to follow. It then becomes increasingly difficult to tread a different path. This analogy demonstrates how habits form and we begin to develop mindsets.

Mindsets are a fixed attitude or disposition that predetermines a person's interpretation of a situation. A classic example of this is stereotyping or pigeon-holing people – at their extreme these mindsets can lead to very destructive attitudes such as racism and sexism.

Other examples include:
×   Seeing people we work with only in terms of their role within the organization
×   Viewing our function or discipline as more important that other people's
×   Preferring to socialize with the same group of people all the time
×   Being unwilling to try food we haven't had before

Some of the phrases that may highlight a mindset are:
×   We tried it before
×   That's not how we do it here
×   It's impossible
×   If it is not broken don't mend it
×   The culture here won't allow that
×   HR won't like that
×   That is against the organization's policy
×   That's not my job

Sometimes shifting our mindsets about things can enable us to make surprising and powerful changes. Looking at our habits and identifying which work for us and which work against us is the first step to changing unproductive patterns

However this is not always easy – if a particular mindset has been developed over many years it can be extremely hard to see things differently.

So how do we ensure that we keep our minds open to change? This has a lot to do with developing flexibility. The more you challenge your mind to see things in different ways the more flexible it becomes.

"The real voyage of discovery consists not in seeing new landscapes but in having new eyes." Marcel Proust

Developing flexible thinking

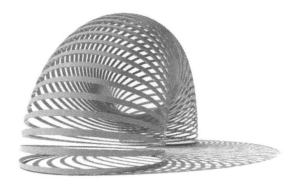

Exercise: Mind puzzles

The following exercises will help you to see how easy you find it to "think outside the box".

1. Connect all nine dots by drawing four straight continuous lines – (without lifting your pencil or re-tracing a line)

$$* \quad * \quad *$$

$$* \quad * \quad *$$

$$* \quad * \quad *$$

2. Add one straight line to make the following true:

$$5 + 5 + 5 = 550$$

3. Decide where the next two letters of the alphabet should be placed to follow the pattern?

$$\frac{A \qquad E\ F \quad H}{B\ C\ D \qquad G}$$

4. Identify two things that you have not eaten before and would like to try.

5. In the next two minutes write down all the uses you can think of for a paperclip.

[Ideas for answers are at the back of the book.]

If you found those difficult you may benefit from trying some of the following things – these are all ideas that help to keep our minds flexible.

✓ Doing crosswords, puzzles or Sudoku
✓ Using brain training software
✓ Listening to music that is completely different to the music you would normally listen to
✓ When you do the shopping buy at least two things that are different
✓ Finding a new way to get to work
✓ Open your mind to other views – think about a controversial issue that you have strong feelings about. Prepare a case defending you opinion with as much evidence as possible. Then prepare another case defending the other side of the argument, again with as much evidence as possible
✓ Spend an hour searching on the internet – put in a topic that interests you and then keep following any links that capture your imagination – keep going and see where it takes you
✓ Try blocking one of your senses – listen to music with your eyes closed, observe a group of people without being able to hear them
✓ Play strategy games like chess or bridge or computer strategy games
✓ Decide to have lunch with different people at work
✓ Read a newspaper that you would not normally read
✓ Visit a museum or art gallery you have not been to before
✓ Watch TV that you would normally avoid – documentary, nature programme, soap, reality show, the news

Exercise: Developing flexible thinking

Review the list above and identify three things that you are going to do to develop your mind's flexibility.

1. ....
2. ....
3. ....

Considering other viewpoints

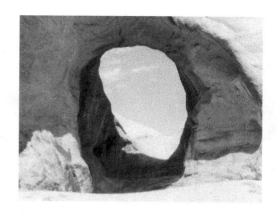

PACE technique

This is a useful technique for stopping and thinking about the other person's viewpoint before jumping to conclusions. It involves four stages:

Pause – do not respond immediately, count to 10 before saying anything.

Ask questions – use one of the questions described in the empathy section to help you really understand the other side of the argument. The purpose of asking skilful questions is to really explore someone else's map of the world.
e.g. Tell me more about......
I had not thought of it in that way, please could you give me more detail?
What leads you to that conclusion?

Choose – decide whether the new information means that you want to change your viewpoint. REMEMBER – truly influential people are willing to be influenced.

Engage - respond.

Next time someone is saying something that you disagree with practice using this technique before you respond.

Seeking feedback

The final part of this trait is an openness to seek, accept and, if necessary, act on feedback from others. The Johari Window is a simple and useful tool for illustrating and helping us to increase our self awareness. It helps us to understand the importance of both self disclosure and feedback in developing our self concept. The Johari window was developed by psychologists Joseph Luft and Harry Ingham in the 1950's. The name came from combining their first names Joe and Harry.

The model represents information about us as a four paned window. The squares divide personal awareness into four different types as illustrated in the diagram below. The lines between the panes are like window blinds that can move as interaction progresses.

	Known to self	Unknown to Self
Known to others	**The Open Area** This area represents information that you know about yourself and that other people know about you. e.g. your name, color of hair etc.	**The Blind Area** This area represents things that other people know about you that are unknown to you. e.g. your tone of voice, the effect your behavior has on others etc.
Unknown to others	**The Hidden Area** This area represents the things that you know about yourself but do not share with others.	**The Unknown Area** This is all the information that is currently unknown to you and to others about you. It is the area that is still to be discovered.

The Johari Window panes can be changed in size. To illustrate this further the diagram below represents an example of the window for a new member to an existing team of people.

	Known to self	**Unknown to Self**
Known to others	The Open Area	The Blind Area
Unknown to others	The Hidden Area	The Unknown Area

In this example the open area is quite small because little is known yet about the new member of the team. Similarly the blind area is small because other people in the team do not know much about the new person yet.

In our experience influential people tend to have a larger open area than any other pane. They are constantly striving to increase this area because they recognize that as it grows so does the level of trust and understanding between them and others.

Here are three ways that we can increase the open area of our window:

Through asking others for feedback – this increases the open area by reducing the blind area. Many people find it difficult to give feedback to others, particularly if they have previously been in a relationship or organization where it was discouraged.

In training workshops participants have identified the following as some examples of ways they have solicited feedback:

✓ Going through a 360 degree appraisal process

✓ At the end of all one to one meetings with their staff a manager asks the question "Is there anything I could do that would make your job easier?"

✓ Ask someone before a meeting or presentation if they would be willing to give you some feedback after the event.

✓ Agreeing that during team meetings if someone makes a contribution the rest of the team will give honest feedback.

✓ Through team development workshops

✓ Getting a coach

✓ Finding a mentor

✓ Joining an action learning set

Through self disclosure – being clear and open with people about how we feel, what we want and what we believe in, helps to reduce the hidden area and thereby makes the open area bigger.

This is not about revealing everything about ourselves as clearly too much information can make others feel uncomfortable. However it is about being willing to share more of you as a relationship develops.

Through reducing the unknown area – This ties back to some of the suggestions about increasing the flexibility of our mind.

Only by opening ourselves up to new experiences will we discover our potential. Influential people are curious and interested to know what they will discover about themselves through new experiences. That curiosity enables them to move beyond the fear of new experience and into the realms of new possibilities.

In her book "Feel The Fear and Do It Anyway", Susan Jeffers encourages us to take more risks. We refer to risk taking in the first chapter as being a positive way to increase your influence. This does not refer to taking risks with health and safety but to taking the kind of risks that help you increase your knowledge of yourself and therefore stretch your mind.

*"If you do what you've always done,
you will always get what you've always got."
Anthony Robbins*

Exercise: Increasing your open area

Self Disclosure:
Identify 3 things that you are currently keeping to yourself but would like to disclose to someone else in order to deepen your relationship with that person. You can choose either one thing to disclose to 3 separate people or 3 things to disclose to the same person.

Write down what those 3 things are and who you intend to disclose them to.
Think about the benefits
How will this piece of self disclosure deepen your relationship with that person/those people?
How will you feel as that relationship becomes better?

1.
2.
3.

As we discussed earlier, we have more credibility and trust and thus more influence with those people who we have strong relationships with. Keeping your relationships at surface level will decrease rather than increase your influence.

New Experiences
Identify 3 new experiences that you would like to engage in. These should be things which will take you out of your comfort zone and enable you to understand more about your potential.
Once again consider the benefits.
How will you feel when you try out something new?
What do you believe it will enable you to discover about yourself?

1.
2.
3.

Summary of trait 7:
Open-mindedness

In summary to develop this trait, concentrate on:

✓ Practicing seeing things from different perspectives

✓ Avoiding the trap of responding too quickly to new ideas and therefore being negative

✓ Reviewing where your habits and mindsets have formed and checking that they are working for you and not against you

✓ Doing things that will help to keep your mind flexible

✓ Using the PACE technique to explore other people's views and to allow yourself time to reflect on whether you want to alter your opinion

✓ Developing ways to get feedback from other people on your impact and presence

Further Reading:

The Mind Map Book, Tony Buzan and Barry Buzan,
BBC Active, 978-1406612790

Feel the Fear and Do It Anyway, Susan Jeffers, Vermillion,
978-0091907075

www.businessballs.com/johariwindowmodel.htm

Increasing your influence:
Personal action plan

"Though no one can go back and make a brand new start,
anyone can start from now
and make a brand new ending."

Increasing your influence:
Personal action plan

The purpose of an action plan is twofold it:

✓ Encourages you to review what you feel you have learned from working through this book

✓ Helps you to commit to some clearly defined actions to transfer those learning points into your everyday life

Action I'm going to take	What is the first step?	When will I take it?

ACTION PLAN

Action I'm going to take	What is the first step?	When will I take it?

Final Thoughts

We hope you have enjoyed your journey through the 7 traits and will feel able to start to practice them in your life from here.

You will already be in possession of some of the traits and will want to strengthen others. Please continue to use the exercises and the further references to expand your understanding and as a starting point to further skill development.

Be patient with yourself, one of the most important things in self development is to allow yourself the time to learn.
Our experience is that becoming more influential is a development journey and we hope that we have given you a pathway to guide you on that journey.

We feel privileged to share our views with you through this book and please contact us if you have questions or feel our work would help you in other ways.

You can find us on

www.spherecreativelearning.com
www.deborahdalley.com

Best Wishes

Lois and Deborah

Answers to the mind puzzles in Trait 7:

The following exercises will help you to see how easy you find it to "think outside the box".

1. Connect all nine dots by drawing four straight continuous lines – (without lifting your pencil or re-tracing a line)

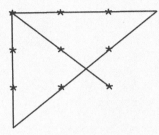

2. You could make the equals sign into not equals:

$$5 + 5 + 5 \neq 550$$

or (there is usually more than one solution) make the first plus into a 4 so the equation reads 545 +5

$$5\ 4\ 5 + 5 = 550$$

3. The top row have all straight lines, the bottom letters have curves.

<pre>
 A   E F H I
   B C D   G   J
</pre>

4. When are you going to try the two foods you chose?

5. Here are just a few ideas for using a paperclip:

Open a letter
Replace a zip
Unclog a Tippex bottle
As a wire in an electric circuit
As an earring
As a weight
To pull a fish along in magnetic fishing game
To pick a lock
To keep your hair in place
As a tooth pick
Clean your nails
Scratch your name on a rock
As money (stranger things have been used)
As a fish hook
Make a hole in something
Melt it down and make a key (a very small one)
What if the paper clip was plastic....
What if it were giant sized and then you melted it - you could make loads of stuff

You could even use it to hold paper together!

Universe of Learning books

"The things I want to know are in books; my best friend is the man who'll get me a book I ain't read."

Abraham Lincoln

About the publishers

Universe of Learning Limited is a small publisher based in the UK with production in England and America. Our authors are all experienced trainers or teachers who have taught their skills for many years. We are actively seeking qualified authors and if you visit the authors section on www.UoLearn.com you can find out how to apply.

If you would like any of our current authors (including Lois www.spherecreativelearning.com and Deborah www.deborahdalley.com) to speak at your event please do visit their own websites or email them through the author section of the UoLearn site.

If you would like to purchase larger numbers of books then please do contact us (sales@UoLearn.com). We give discounts from 5 books upwards. For larger volumes we can also quote for changes to the cover to accommodate your company logo and to the interior to brand it for your company.

All our books are written by teachers, trainers or people well experienced in their roles and our goal is to help people develop their skills with a well structured range of exercises.

If you have any feedback about this book or other topics that you'd like to see us cover please do contact us at support@UoLearn.com.

Keep Learning!

Coaching Skills Training Course

Your toolkit to coaching yourself and others, with exercises and scripts

ISBN: 978-1-84937-019-6, Order at www.UoLearn.com

This book gives you an easy to follow structure to design inspiring coaching sessions.

- ✓ An easy to follow 5 step model to guide you through the coaching process.
- ✓ Exercises will help you enhance your skills
- ✓ Work at your own pace to increase your ability
- ✓ How to use NLP in your coaching
- ✓ Over 25 ready to use ideas

A toolbox of ideas to help you become a great coach.

Speed Writing
Skills Training Course

Speedwriting for faster note taking and dictation, an alternative to shorthand to help you take notes.

Easy exercises to learn faster writing in just 6 hours. Free downloadable Dictionary and Workbook.

ISBN 978-1-84937-011-0, from www.UoLearn.com

- ✓ "The principles are very easy to follow, and I am already using it to take notes."
- ✓ "BakerWrite is the easiest shorthand system I have come across. Having studied all the major shorthand systems and other speed writing courses, I find BakerWrite a sheer delight."
- ✓ "I will use this system all the time."
- ✓ "Your system is so easy to learn and use."

Speed Reading Skills Training Course

How to read a book, report or short document on paper or online three times as fast with comprehension for study skills and business

Free downloadable speed reading test and workbook
Easy exercises and software reviews to learn rapid reading

ISBN: 978-1-84937-021-9, Order at www.UoLearn.com

Would you like to learn simple techniques to help you read 3 times as fast?
This book has a series of easy to follow guided exercises that help you change your reading habits to both read faster and to evaluate which parts to read and in what order.

Stress Management Skills Training Course

Exercises and techniques to identify the symptoms of stress and anxiety. Build success in your life by goal setting, relaxation and changing thinking with NLP

Free downloadable workbook

ISBN: 978-1-84937-024-0, Order at www.UoLearn.com

✓ Identify the symptoms of stress and anxiety

✓ Use easy techniques to change your thinking

✓ Simple exercises to help you relax

✓ Build your life around success

CPSIA information can be obtained
at www.ICGtesting.com
Printed in the USA
LVHW060222271020
669922LV00007B/54